*Integrative Brief Therapy*

# Publisher's Note

*Books in "The Practical Therapist Series" present authoritative answers to the question, "what-do-I-do-now-and-how-do-I-do-it?" in the practice of psychotherapy, bringing the wisdom and experience of expert mentors to the practicing therapist. A book, however, is no substitute for thorough professional training and adherence to ethical and legal standards. At minimum:*

- *The practitioner must be qualified to practice psychotherapy.*
- *Clients participate in psychotherapy only with informed consent.*
- *The practitioner must not "guarantee" a specific outcome.*

— Robert E. Alberti, Ph.D.

# Integrative Brief Therapy

## Cognitive, Psychodynamic, Humanistic & Neurobehavioral Approaches

John Preston, Psy.D.

**The Practical Therapist Series™**

**Impact Publishers®**
SAN LUIS OBISPO, CALIFORNIA 93406

Copyright © 1998
by John Preston

Impact Publishers and colophon are registered trademarks of Impact Publishers, Inc.

ATTENTION ORGANIZATIONS AND CORPORATIONS:
This book is available at quantity discounts on bulk purchases for educational, business, or sales promotional use. For further information, please contact Impact Publishers, P.O. Box 910, San Luis Obispo, CA 93406-0910 (Phone: 1-800-246-7228).

**Library of Congress Cataloging-in-Publication Data**

Preston, John, 1950-
    Integrative brief therapy : cognitive, psychodynamic, humanistic,
and neurobehavioral approaches / John Preston.
      p.    cm. -- (The practical therapist series)
    Includes bibliographical references and index.
    ISBN 1--886230-09-9 (alk. paper)
    1. Brief psychotherapy. 2. Eclectic psychotherapy.    I. Title.
II. Series.
    RC480.55.P735    1998
    616.89'14--dc21                        98.7498
                                           CIP

Cover design by Sharon Schnare, San Luis Obispo, California
Printed in the United States of America on acid-free paper
Published by **Impact ☒ Publishers®**
POST OFFICE BOX 910
SAN LUIS OBISPO, CALIFORNIA 93406-0910

# Dedication

*To Bonnie — my wife and best friend*

# TABLE OF CONTENTS

## Integrative Brief Therapy

# Acknowledgements

With deep appreciation for the contributions of Carl Rogers, who so eloquently taught us of the importance of empathy and love as *the* critical components in healing relationships. In an era of quick fix technologies may we never lose sight of what matters most in this most intimate of human relationships.

Many thanks to my very capable publisher and colleague, Dr. Robert Alberti; thank you for your faith in me. Gratitude to Rachel Youngman, who provided tremendous help in editing and to Michelle Riekstins for her usual superb assistance in manuscript preparation. And, as always, what a pleasure to work with such wonderful people: the Impact Publishers staff. You're great!

I also wish to acknowledge the pioneering work of the following psychotherapists and researchers: Dr. Martin Seligman, Dr. Hans Strupp, Dr. Albert Bandura, and Dr. David Shapiro.

Heartfelt thanks to those who have encouraged me in my writing and clinical work over the years: Dr. Jay Adams, Dr. Mac Sterling, Dr. Douglas Hooker, Dr. Corinne Giantonio, and Dr. Matt McKay.

And finally, I would like to express my sincere gratitude to my students and psychotherapy clients.

# PREFACE

## *The Challenge*

Brief therapy may be clearly indicated with certain clients, for some, it is the treatment of choice. However, in these times of managed care, often brief therapy is not chosen, it is mandated by HMO's, EAP's, or third party payers. Great. So here we are with the task of providing brief treatment for all sorts of people. Some of these folks may be ideal brief therapy candidates, but many are not. Just because it may *seem* cost effective to offer shorter-term treatment, in no way does that guarantee that brief therapy is really clinically indicated in a number of cases.

So, given this challenge, what are we to do? In this book I will argue that if we are to stand any chance of accomplishing the task of providing successful brief therapy, we must be able to assess clients rapidly and then choose *specific* intervention strategies that have the greatest likelihood of accomplishing our treatment goals (and that the choice of interventions, rather than being directed by a therapist's theory of choice or ideology *de jour* should come directly from our assessment of the client). Specifically, the most crucial assessment question will be, *"What does this particular client need at this point in his or her life to heal, to grow, or to cope more effectively?"* Since the kind of problems people have are so diverse, in my opinion, this requires that therapists have at their disposal a number of intervention strategies, and that no one theoretical model can adequately address the vast array of problems our clients present to us. I do not think that I am alone in this belief, since the idea of drawing from a number of theoretical models has recently caught the attention of many clinicians and authors.

This book is written to address such concerns. We start off by considering a number of basic issues regarding psychopathology, adaptation, and healing. Then we move into a discussion of assessment, and finally we explore a set of specific treatment strategies, drawn from several important schools of psychotherapy.

"*Facts without values, fragmentary specialties with no integrating philosophy of life as a whole, data with no ethical standards for their use, techniques... with no convictions about life's ultimate meaning... here a panacea has turned out to be a problem.*"
— Harry Emerson Fosdick
*The Living of These Days* (1956)

# Introduction

*"What the hell am I supposed to do now?!"*

After several years of graduate school, I met with my first psychotherapy clients. If one of them had asked me to write a term paper or to define a psychological concept, I would have come through with flying colors. But my confidence went only so far. Often in those first days of my new career — and many, many times since then — I've had moments while in therapy sessions, silently wondering, "What the hell am I supposed to do now?!" Solid intellectual grounding in processes such as clarification and interpretation and understanding (at least in general) such phenomena as transference did little to guide me in the moment. I often felt lost.

Books written about chess say a lot regarding opening-move strategies and also about how to deal with the game in its closing stages. However, aside from general suggestions, little advice is offered for the middle (and by far the most extensive) aspects of a game of chess. The same applies to books regarding psychotherapy. I assume that I was like many other beginning therapists: I very much wanted some direction to help guide me once therapy was underway, but I was hard pressed to find direction in the myriad of available psychotherapy texts. That is why I decided to write this book.

I am hopeful that it can provide some guidelines for *general* treatment strategies, as well as ways to help the clinician decide how to proceed, moment to moment, as therapy progresses.

As a graduate student in the early 1970s I observed theoretical shoot-outs, as proponents from various schools of thought amassed persuasive arguments (and sometimes research) to demonstrate that their particular approach was the best. Behaviorists presented impressive data to highlight their treatment successes. (Especially noteworthy were high cure rates among college students with snake phobias — a psychological disorder of almost epidemic magnitude, if measured by the volume of studies on the subject!) Psychodynamic writers, who had few empirical data to back up their claims, retorted that critical psychological problems, like an underdeveloped sense of self or ego weakness, were too subtle and complicated to be measured precisely (explaining their lack of research support). And ultimately these psychological problems should be considered more important and legitimate concerns in the practice of psychotherapy than simple phobias. Who was right and who was wrong? Which approach yielded better outcomes?

Fortunately, psychotherapy outcome research blossomed. Hundreds of studies looked not only at outcome per se, but also began to look at the nuances of the therapeutic processes (e.g., numerous client variables, including motivation, psychological mindedness, and likability; therapists variables, such as the degree of empathic understanding or rigidity; and exhaustive analyses of moment-to-moment interactions as recorded on video tape). Theoretical debate continued but was softened somewhat by the results of large-scale studies (meta-analyses) that, for the first time, demonstrated rather strongly that no particular model of psychotherapy was especially superior to another. These studies yielded three general conclusions: (1) Overall, the majority of outcome studies did demonstrate that psychotherapy is effective (for a large variety of psychological disorders); (2) Although the majority of clients benefit from therapy, some do not, and a minority of clients get worse (i.e., either the therapy was not able to halt further decompensation and/or the treatment itself was harmful to the clients); and (3) In head-to-head comparisons, no single type of psychotherapy emerged as clearly superior; although behavioral treatments had somewhat better outcomes than psychodynamic models, the difference was not statistically significant.

As the "who-has-the-best-theoretical-model" debate continued, other researchers shifted their focus away from particular theoretical approaches, to study important personal characteristics of therapists and styles of therapeutic interaction. Most notably, Yalom (1995) indicated that regardless of one's theoretical persuasion, it is likely that the personality style and personal characteristics of the therapist may be *the* decisive variables that account for therapeutic success.

To expand on these findings, the pioneering work of Jerome Frank (1973) presented an interesting illustration of common features seen in a multitude of healing relationships (not only various forms of conventional psychotherapy, but also faith-healing and rituals of shamen and witch doctors). In summary, Frank and other writers in the 1970s delineated a number of common characteristics that appear to be necessary (and maybe sufficient) to promote psychological healing (see sidebar page 4). To a greater or lesser degree, all these factors are evident in psychotherapies from various theoretical perspectives.

## *Common Features in Psychotherapies*

1. The therapist creates a helping relationship that is characterized by safety, caring, respect, support, privacy,and trust (Strupp, 1969, 1973). It is in the context of an intense, confiding relationship that psychological growth and healing can best occur (Frank, 1973).
2. Therapists are guided by a set of theoretical assumptions or rationales, and particular techniques from which they are derived (Frank, 1973).
3. Successful therapists are capable of fostering hope and of transmitting realistic expectations of being helped, so crucial in combating demoralization (Frank, 1973).
4. The client must be willing and able to enter treatment and to a degree allow for some amount of human contact (in order for this relationship to have an impact) (Strupp, 1969, 1973).
5. Behavioral change generally does not occur in an emotional vacuum, thus successful therapies, to some extent must occur in the context of optimal emotional arousal (Frank, 1973).
6. Therapists of varying theoretical persuasions (to a greater or lesser degree) influence behavioral changes by the following methods (the specific techniques employed vary a good deal from one model to another, but the basic principles and outcomes are similar):
   a. The transmission of new information (e.g., to promote gaining new perspectives or developing greater clarity about important life events or inner values, beliefs, feelings, and needs) (Strupp, 1969, 1973; Frank, 1973).
   b. Reconditioning (e.g., reducing anxiety associated with certain situations or decreasing one's sense of shame when talking about personal issues) (Chessick, 1969, 1974).
   c. Providing success experiences (which enhance a sense of mastery and increased self-esteem).
   d. Modeling: This may be done explicitly as in certain behavior therapies (e.g., exposure treatment for OCD or assertiveness training) or implicitly (e.g., the therapist may serve as a model for the client, for example, by his or her willingness to face painful feelings with courage or without self-criticism).
   e. Repeated reality testing: Encouraging the client to take a close look at situations, events, relationships, and one's own inner "truths" (to see inner and outer realities more clearly).
   f. Promoting the release of tension (catharsis) (Chessick, 1969, 1974).
   g. Providing a "corrective experience" in the relationship: As the client gradually may come to see that the therapist does not repeat hurtful patterns of interaction with him or her, or sensing on a deep level that the therapist genuinely cares for and respects the client.

These factors may turn out to be more important than one's particular theoretical frame of reference or repertoire of technical interventions.

Finally, and maybe most important, are the findings reported by Carl Rogers and colleagues (1961). Rogers's research isolated and illuminated three critical variables that most current therapists of various schools of thought agree are essential ingredients in successful therapists.

---

### Rogers's Necessary and Sufficient Ingredients That Characterize the Therapist's Attitude

- **Genuineness:** a quality of honesty and sincerity.
- **Unconditional Positive Regard:** a communication of the therapist's deep and genuine concern and care for the client, expressed in a nonevaluative manner.
- **Accurate Empathic Understanding:** a moment-to-moment sensitivity to the client, the ability to accurately understand or resonate with the client, and to clearly transmit empathic understanding to the client.

\* More psychodynamically oriented therapists have emphasized an atmosphere of *neutrality.* It is important to underscore that neutrality does not mean an uninvolved stance — quite the contrary. True neutrality means the ability to be open to hearing and understanding the client without criticism or judgment.

---

In addition to Rogers's particular ideas regarding theory and techniques of therapy, his most lasting contribution to the field may have been his philosophy of therapy. He believed strongly in the inherent good in people and an innate striving toward emotional health and growth. He also believed that if healing and self-actualization are to occur, a decent, compassionate, and empathic relationship is the most powerful catalyst for change.

*Multiple working hypotheses diminish the danger of*
*parental affection for our favorite theory offspring.*
        — Harry Wilmer, *Practical Jung*

Something has become clear, especially in recent years. The terrain of human psychological functioning is so complex that single models or techniques are often inadequate. Most attempts to develop an overarching model to explain all human behavior have fallen short of the mark. This is probably one reason that much current effort and interest have been directed toward developing *integrated models of psychotherapy.*

People become wedded to their theories and this happens for understandable reasons. Theories provide at least two things. First, they are conceptual maps. Theories help therapists to understand what otherwise might be extremely complicated or confusing behaviors and symptoms. They also — one hopes — give us guidelines on how to proceed and what to do. Theories, ultimately, are only useful if they can translate into successful action plans. A second goal of theories is to help the therapist feel more confident; they provide us with some sense of security. An old joke states that the psychoanalyst in training commented, "Even if the patient doesn't get better, at least I know I am doing the right thing." Feeling at least somewhat confident is not only desirable as this relates to the therapist's own sense of security, but also may be helpful for the client. If a person is in a good deal of emotional pain or desperation, it is reassuring to see that the therapist sitting across the room seems to know what he or she is doing. It can help engender a sense of hope, which is an important experience for all psychotherapy clients.

In the best of circumstances, good theories accomplish both: helping the therapist feel reasonably confident and providing a good map to guide and direct understanding and successful interventions.

Research data and persuasive writings certainly influence graduate students, psychiatry residents, and practicing clinicians. However, I suspect that ultimately the therapeutic model therapists endorse has much more to do with their own internal values and life experiences (especially beliefs about emotional suffering, healing, growth, and human interactions). In my view, it is very important for all therapists to do some soul-searching and to get clear about their own inner values and beliefs. Ultimately being true to yourself and in that way interacting with clients in an authentic way, may have much more to do with successful therapy than memorizing the particulars of a certain theoretical model.

At the same time, I also believe that it is important to become acquainted with various therapeutic models. The main reason for this is simply that human psychological problems are so very complex. There is an old saying, "If the only tool you have is a hammer, then all problems start looking like nails." A therapist is likely to need a number of approaches at his/her disposal when confronted with a wide variety of client problems. And yet, therapeutic interventions should not be used in some kind of arbitrary form of eclecticism.

In this book we look at four complementary models. In recent years it has become more and more popular for therapists to develop hybrids of more classical approaches, primarily because to do so can facilitate more effective treatment. I have chosen to include cognitive-behavioral, humanistic, and psychodynamic models as the dominant approaches, and also to address neurobiology, as we attempt to map out the territory and some specific strategies for conducting psychological treatment. Although we start with some theory, the main thrust of the book is an applied, nuts-and-bolts guide to psychotherapy. I have wanted to write a book that is straightforward and understandable. I sincerely hope you will find it helpful.

### ❖ *Summary*

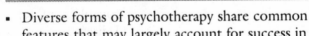

- Diverse forms of psychotherapy share common features that may largely account for success in treatment, independent of the particular theoretical orientation.

- Genuineness, positive regard, and accurate empathic understanding are core elements in healing relationships.

# PART ONE

*Assumptions*

## Basic Assumptions

L et's get started by considering the following assumption. Often life is hard, and *sooner or later, every person will encounter difficulties.* This will include, at the very least, facing losses as, for example, friends or loved ones move away or die, and encountering developmental challenges, such as having to come to terms with the effects of aging, existential issues, and a host of other common experiences that life presents. The three major tasks for every human being are (1) to deal with difficult life circumstances (to cope as well as possible), (2) to do one's best to recover and heal in the aftermath of painful events, and (3) to grow. Emotional growth, of course, involves a number of developmental aspects, with the establishment of a *self* taking center stage.

Let's consider a second assumption: *All people are not created equal.* The challenges of emotional healing and personal growth must be faced by all, but each person brings to these situations his or her own unique set of strengths and liabilities. On the optimal end of the spectrum are those blessed with (1) *good biology* (well-developed, intact nervous systems free from significant medical disorders or physical handicaps); (2) *good enough early experiences* in their family of origin, which contribute to the development of personal talents, adequate ego strengths, and positive characterological attributes; and (3) *good luck in life* (actually good luck combined with skillful living and wise choices of career and friends). These three areas are what psychiatrist James Masterson refers to as the effects of nature, nurture, and fate.

In a simplistic way, which is a good place to start, we can consider that any noticeable deviation from optimal circumstances in any or all of the three areas may result in some compromised psychological functioning. When there are minor glitches, the result will typically be seen in the form of barely noticeable problems or quirks of personality, and minor adjustment disorders. However, with more strikes against a person, in any of the three areas, we are likely to see more personality dysfunction, less than optimal coping abilities, and/or the emergence of more intense suffering (i.e., symptomatology). Rather than seeing the various forms of psychiatric disorders simply as discrete entities, we may consider a spectrum of personality function that ranges from optimal to grossly dysfunctional. One way to illustrate this is by way of Figure 2-A. The three dimensions captured in this diagram are: first, the *level of personality functioning*. This refers to one's level of emotional maturity and ego

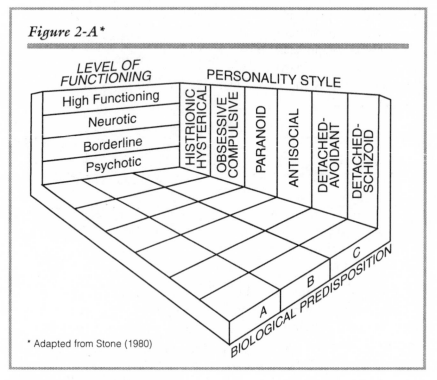

*Figure 2-A**

* Adapted from Stone (1980)

## Biological Predispositions
*A: No evidence of biologic diathesis*
*B: Generalized neurobiologic problem*
*C: Specific Neuropsychiatric Disorder (e.g. Panic Disorder, Bi-polar)*

functioning in general — the particular set of strengths and weaknesses that the person carries through adult life. (Of course, this is subject to change over time as a consequence of either severe or ongoing stresses, or, conversely, in a positive vein, continued growth. However, for the time being, let's assume that this axis on the diagram represents a fairly stable level of functioning.) The next dimension reflects the *presence or absence of a neurobiological diathesis*. This may be a long-standing problem in the nervous system due to constitutional or temperamental factors, inadequate neurological development, or the effects of disease or trauma on the brain, which leaves the individual impaired in his or her cognitive and/or affective control abilities. It may be an underlying predisposition for the development of a neurobiological psychiatric disorder, for example, bipolar disorder or schizophrenia. The third dimension pertains to the individual's predominant personality style (characterized by particular approaches to coping, the use of certain defense mechanisms, cognitive and affective style, and so forth).

Beyond the tripartite model, an important fourth dimension reflects the *current level of psychosocial stressors* (see Figure 2-B).

---

### Figure 2-B                                   *Psycho social Stressors*

| Minimal Stressors | | | | Severe and/or Chronic Stressors | | |
|---|---|---|---|---|---|---|
| 1 | 2 | 3 | 4 | 5 | 6 | 7 |

---

Stressors indicated on this axis include both recent stressors and the cumulative effects of ongoing, persistent stressors (e.g., living in extreme poverty, enduring significant, chronic pain, or being subject to ongoing psychological or physical abuse).

A good deal of the focus in psychiatric diagnosis and treatment is on symptoms and the treatment of symptom disorders. This certainly is the case reflected in the *Diagnostic and Statistical Manual of Mental Disorders* (DSM) and is evident in the recent proliferation of treatment *protocols* that are designed to outline specific steps for treating particular disorders (e.g., panic disorder or depression). I am very much in favor of these approaches. They have contributed a great deal to the development of standardized nomenclature and thus to better research (since we now have a more mutually agreed on language). And, treatment protocols have been shown to offer excellent guidelines for the therapy of specific disorders (see sidebar page 13). However, in many cases when people come for mental health treatment, the presenting problems do not fit into neat diagnostic packages. This is the case because many people present with mixed *DSM* Axis I disorders (e.g., anxiety and depression ). But, even more commonly, psychotherapists are confronted by people who have a host of very unique problems that can only be appreciated as an amalgamation of characterological problems, coping deficiencies, mistaken assumptions, deeply held maladaptive beliefs, and possible underlying neurobiological dysfunctions. These are complex problems not easily characterized by a single *DSM* diagnosis nor easily addressed by standard treatment protocols. These are the people we see day in and day out in clinical practice.

I would like to propose a way of conceptualizing this. For each person we see for treatment we may ask the following: *"Why isn't life working for this person at this time?" "What are the particular problems and causes that we can identify that contribute to the current predicament?"* and *"What are the specific assets and liabilities that this person is bringing in that can either be used in the service of growth and healing or, conversely, may be interfering with these processes?"* These questions and this perspective do not in any way ignore or minimize the importance of being alert to more circumscribed symptom disorders. When these are present, particular psychotherapy protocols or targeted pharma-cological treatments are certainly in order. However, the proposed perspective encourages the therapist to attend to fundamental questions that can guide him or her to making critical treatment decisions, the most important of which is, *"What does this person need at this time in life that can make a difference in helping him or her to suffer less, to cope more effectively, and to heal and grow?"* As we see in later chapters, this question can be framed in at least two ways. The first is,

## *Psychotherapy Treatment Protocols*

Treatment protocols are standardized psychotherapy guidelines that have been developed for use in the treatment of specific symptom disorders (e.g., panic disorder, obsessive-compulsive disorder, social phobia, etc.). Protocols generally are based on specific time-limited interventions that have been demonstrated to be effective in carefully controlled research trials. The majority of such protocols recommend behavioral and cognitive behavioral interventions. They also rely heavily on the use of homework assignments carried out by the client between therapy sessions. Here is a sample outline for development of a typical protocol:

### Session One:
- Obtain history and conduct comprehensive assessment
- Make a diagnosis and share impressions with the client
- Provide client with an overview of the recommended treatment. (This takes a psychoeducational approach that provides an easy-to-understand explanation of the disorder and rationale for the treatment. One issue that is emphasized is the role of between-sessions homework.)
- The number of anticipated sessions is discussed, and the next appointment is scheduled
- Homework (if appropriate at this stage) is assigned...

### Session Five:
- An agenda is set for the session
- Review of events of the week with special attention given to homework assignments
- New techniques are introduced to supplement already existing approaches (e.g., teaching the use of breathing techniques in the treatment of panic disorder) ...

### Final Session:
- Review of the events of the week and homework assignments
- Take stock of the changes that have occurred during treatment with special attention given to "what has worked," i.e., making it clear that the client's newly developed skills and efforts have been responsible for the reduction of symptoms (the intent is to increase the likelihood that the client will feel a sense of personal mastery and will continue to use certain techniques independently after therapy has ended).

*"What does our client need from therapy in a general sense?"* This question addresses an overarching treatment strategy that can serve as a point of general reference as we embark on treatment with a particular client. In addition, there is the second ongoing question, *"And what does our client need in this moment for therapy to be effective and to progress?"* Obviously, these can be complicated questions. I hope to lay out in the chapters that follow specific ways of organizing our thinking around these questions, and then move on to show how specific treatment interventions can be designed to accomplish our goals.

To begin this, let us first look at a number of assumptions regarding emotional healing and some basic theoretical issues that shed light on the nature of psychological processes and psychopathology. My hope is that a discussion of these issues will lay a foundation for the chapters that follow, which address practical aspects of diagnosis and treatment.

❖
### *Summary*

- People encounter three ongoing challenges while navigating through life: coping, healing, and growth of the self. Psychotherapies aim to facilitate one or more of these essential tasks.

- Accurate understanding of our clients requires not a single model or perspective. Rather, the therapist must be able to appreciate the client from a multitude of perspectives.

- The key questions to address in each and every case are:

    *"Why isn't life working for this person at this time?"*

    *"What are the particular problems and causes that we can identify that contribute to the current predicament?"*

    *"What does our client need from therapy in a general sense, and what does the client need in this moment for therapy to be effective and to progress?"*

3

---

# The Nature of Human
# Emotional Suffering

A useful way to consider emotional suffering is to distinguish between *necessary* and *unnecessary pain* (Peck, 1978; Johnson, 1985; Preston, 1993). *Necessary pain* includes fundamental core emotional reactions to distressing life events. These are the almost-inevitable responses to experiences such as tragic losses, major disappointments, being attacked (emotionally or physically), or enduring physical pain. Such emotional pain can be considered to be "necessary" in two respects. First, it is a natural, normal, healthy expression of suffering seen universally across a multitude of cultures. Certainly each society or subculture influences the particular way that emotions are expressed (i.e., in keeping with prevailing social norms regarding acceptable, sanctioned behavior). But in a basic way, all humans appear to respond to loss with sadness, to being assaulted or attacked with either fear or counteraggression, and to threats to safety or security with fear or anxiety (the list of fundamental human emotions includes seven basic classes of response (noted in Figure 3-A). Some of these core emotional reactions are also seen in nonhuman primates (Izard, 1971; Tomkins, 1962).

A second characteristic of necessary pain is the assumption (one I endorse in this book) that the expression of certain emotions in the aftermath of painful

---

*Figure 3-A*                                    *Basic Human Emotions*

---

Happiness        Fear          Anger
Surprise         Shame         Disgust
                               Sadness

---

life events may be a critical ingredient in facilitating emotional healing. One common example is that the majority of people following major losses move through a rather prolonged experience of sadness and mourning that is experienced largely in private, and at times shared with others. However, some individuals massively overdefend against experiencing the sadness and other emotions resulting from the loss of a loved one. If this is done to an extreme and for an extended period of time, three consequences are often seen: (1) On a deep, unconscious level, the loss is not truly faced or worked through. This may translate into behavioral inhibition, as the person comes to adopt a style of avoiding meaningful contact with others (if you don't get attached, you won't ever experience additional losses). The unresolved, inner wound leads to a maladaptive style of life that may become a permanent fixture in the individual's character. (2) When people psychologically grit their teeth, and overdefend, one frequent consequence is the emergence of psychosomatic symptoms. (3) Those with unresolved issues involving loss become sensitized to subsequent experiences of loss and also appear to be more vulnerable to depression.

When people have access to inner emotions and can give themselves permission to express and share such feelings (at least to a degree), this process may play an important role in emotional recovery. It is probably not a coincidence that almost all cultures have evolved or developed bereavement rituals, most of which encourage open acknowledgment of sadness and loss.

Conversely, *unnecessary pain* is a version of emotional suffering that is extremely common and, unfortunately, quite unhealthy. This is a source of emotional misery that extends beyond necessary pain. It is usually manifest in the tendency for people, in the wake of painful events, to launch into a ruthless attack on the self:

*"What the hell is wrong with me?!"*
*"I'm so stupid."*
*"I can't do anything right."*
*"I'm just a damned loser!"*

In addition to the inevitable emotional pain associated with difficult life circumstances, many of our clients will be seen to engage in various forms of excessive self-criticism or even self-hatred. This kind of pain not only does not facilitate healing; the opposite is true — it is a major source of increased misery.

One primary focus in psychotherapy is to intervene in particular ways to disrupt or reduce various sources of unnecessary pain, while simultaneously helping our clients to acknowledge, honor, and express these legitimate and necessary inner experiences of human suffering. (This is explored in greater detail in following chapters).

### ❖ *In the Eye of the Beholder*

The theory of *observer bias* (Nisbett, et al., 1973) holds that the understanding of human emotional responses can vary tremendously depending on the perspective from which it is viewed. A man is irritated and voices curt, somewhat hostile comments toward a clerk in a store. It is likely that bystanders may think, "What's wrong with that guy?" or, "What an angry person!" The response reflects an assumption that the emotional display is a reflection of the man's character; that is, he is an "angry person." However, the man himself is quite likely to view this event in an entirely different manner. For example, he would be much less inclined to see himself as an angry person, and rather, if asked, would justify his reactions in terms of what seems to be a reasonable explanation: "I've been treated badly by this store and anyone would be understandably upset." Or, "I've had a terrible week. My teenage son is using drugs, I'm on the edge financially, and now all I am trying to do is to return a defective product to the store, and this clerk is not being helpful or cooperative."

This model highlights the fact that many people are prone to make conclusions about others based on scant data, and often such conclusions are pejorative. This, of course, involves making a *judgment* about the other, rather than attempting to understand the whole picture. Emotional reactions and other observable behaviors are clearly influenced by characterological factors, but are also almost always in response to numerous situational variables. When people take the time to inquire and attempt to understand what is really going on in any situation, most times emotional responses can be better understood as arising out of a host of factors. Knowing something about the context (e.g., recent events) as well as uniquely personal factors (e.g., the man's history, his personality style, his particular area of emotional vulnerability, and his perception of the current situation) will give us a better shot at truly understanding another's reactions.

### ❖ The "Pain" and the "Problem"

As clients present themselves for psychotherapy, they reveal a great deal for therapists to consider. They share recent life events, their concerns, symptoms, inhibitions; we get glimpses of their histories and come to know about their particular character style (both assets and liabilities). From this flow of information therapists must struggle to make sense of what we see.

One helpful guideline is to attempt to differentiate two issues: the client's pain and the client's problem.

The "pain" refers to the core human emotions associated with painful life experiences. Returning to two earlier examples, the man in the store is worried about his son, he is distressed about his finances, and he is frustrated and irritated as he encounters problems in returning merchandise to the store. His "problem," however, may be that as he faces these struggles in his life, he has not spoken to his wife or friends about his feelings. He may not have developed the ability to open up comfortably to another, thus, he frets and worries in the isolation of his own mind. He has an underdeveloped capacity to understand his inner emotional self, and thus, when confronted with tense encounters with his son, he is beset by vague feelings of uneasiness and frustration, not at all aware of deeper feelings of love for his son and worries about his welfare. An additional part of his "problem" is that he has not been able to develop the ability for introspection or psychological mindedness that might otherwise serve him in coming to terms with current difficulties.

The person who is excessively blocked from her grief after the death of her husband internally harbors feelings of sadness and loss. However, on a more conscious level she is attempting to "get on with her life." As she experiences tension headaches, insomnia, and fatigue, her ability to function at work begins to slip. She often thinks, "I'm just screwing up too much. What the hell is wrong with me?!" Her "problem" is *not* that she has lost her husband (that is a tragic event and accounts for her buried sadness). The problems are that she is not in touch with the truth of inner emotions, she is not grieving her loss, she has developed stress-related somatic symptoms, and she is now quite prone to engaging in a good deal of self-criticism.

It may be helpful, as we encounter each psychotherapy client, to ask ourselves, "What is his pain and what are his problems?" This question may be useful in sorting out these two factors that are so commonly seen in our clients: legitimate human suffering, and issues (dynamics, defenses, and coping strategies) that are interfering with the capacity to come to terms with difficult life circumstances.

❖ *Summary*
═══════════════════════════════════════════

- It is important to be able to distinguish between *necessary pain* and *unnecessary pain* to be able to appreciate that certain types of emotional suffering may be a necessary part of the human condition and essential to experience for healing and growth to occur. Certain types of pain, however, lead to unnecessary misery and retard growth and healing; such pain is a target for eradication.

- An important distinction must be made between a person's "pain" (core human suffering) and his or her "problems" (psychological liabilities that interfere with growth or healing).

# 4

## Understanding Emotional Healing Under Optimal Circumstances

As a practicing psychotherapist, you'll need to develop a working model that helps to explain how people heal in the aftermath of difficult or tragic life events or cope more effectively with the stresses of everyday experience. How does emotional healing occur? What processes promote or enhance recovery from painful life experiences? Although obviously there are tremendous differences among people's styles of dealing with emotional distress, there also appear to be some remarkable commonalities. Let's take a look.

During the early part of the twentieth century, Sigmund Freud was beginning to develop the basic foundations of psychoanalysis. He had already forged many of the early theoretical ideas of his emerging school of thought when World War I began. As a medical officer in the Austrian military, Freud was responsible for treating a number of soldiers suffering from what was then called "shell shock." (More recently this has been referred to as post-traumatic stress disorder.) In his private practice prior to the war, Freud had been fascinated by the variety and uniqueness of his patients' problems — their particular symptoms, histories, and unconscious conflicts. But his wartime experience made him aware of a multitude of emotional problems that appeared not unique, but rather quite stereotyped and predictable. Almost regardless of the soldiers' personality styles or backgrounds, countless hundreds of them returned from the front suffering from remarkably similar psychological symptoms. They had a tendency to move back and forth between two seemingly opposite states of mind: from tremendous emotional upheaval (e.g., anxiety, trembling, fearfulness, crying) to withdrawal (numbness, distance, and lack of emotion).

These World War I combat veterans also showed two additional symptoms. The first was *a tendency to repetitively recall horrific, traumatic events;* their conscious minds were flooded by these memories. They frequently relived the traumatic experiences, in waking hours and in recurring nightmares. They were troubled by intense emotions when recalling the traumatic events, and they actively attempted to suppress the memories. The second symptom was a *variety of physical complaints* for which no organic cause could be determined. Headaches, insomnia, abdominal pain, and poor appetite — symptoms now understood to be psychosomatic — were mysterious to Freud and his fellow military doctors 75 years ago.

Freud's patients returning from the front by-and-large were not people with mental illnesses; they were relatively normal people who had been exposed to extremely severe stress. This same rather stereotyped reaction pattern has been seen in subsequent wars, and was brought into public awareness most notably following the Vietnam War.

Twenty-five years later, Eric Lindeman, a psychiatric researcher and clinician, had the opportunity again to observe and study closely the effects of severe stress on normal people. In 1942, during a post-football celebration at the Coconut Grove nightclub in Boston, a disastrous fire claimed the lives of 499 people and stunned the community. Lindeman and his colleagues quickly rushed in and provided free counseling services for a large group of people, including survivors of the fire and relatives of the victims. The researchers established what amounted to the first community-based mental health intervention in the country. At the same time the mental health team was able to study carefully this group of people. Like the soldiers in Freud's studies, by-and-large, these were normal people caught up in the wake of disaster. Lindeman, too, discovered considerable regularity in the symptoms that people reported: the vacillation between overwhelming painful emotions and periods of numbness; a strong need or impulse to repeat the tragic events in their minds over and over again; a host of psychosomatic symptoms.

Prior to the 1950s, many theories regarding emotional stress and psychiatric symptoms were developed, primarily from experience in treating severely mentally ill people. Little was really understood about emotional distress among relatively normal people. However, the observations of Freud, Lindeman, and subsequent researchers were beginning to shed light on what might be a rather general pattern of responses to significant emotional stress.

### ❖ The Stress Response Syndrome

In 1976, psychiatrist Mardi Horowitz wrote a book entitled *Stress Response Syndromes.* In this landmark publication, Horowitz carved out a very useful model for understanding what appears to be a common pattern of human emotional response to significant stress. Horowitz developed this model based on his review of numerous field studies (like that of Lindeman), a good deal of clinical work treating mentally healthy people who had experienced major stresses, and even some experimental studies. The studies included, among others, research with college students in which the volunteer subjects were exposed to fairly intense, stressful movies (e.g., films of Nazi concentration camps). Horowitz concluded that across a broad spectrum of stressful events (death of loved ones, physical assaults, natural disasters, and even viewing upsetting movies), most people exhibit a typical pattern of response; what he termed the "stress response syndrome." This model can be helpful in understanding common human reactions to stressful events. And, as we will explore later, embedded in this model are some important keys to understanding the emotional healing process.

Let's take a look at the stress response syndrome. The full stress response syndrome is seen most clearly in situations where the stressful event is sudden and intense. Although a host of events may trigger this reaction, we'll use the example of a sudden loss (e.g., the death of a loved one). Less intense or less sudden stressors also elicit similar

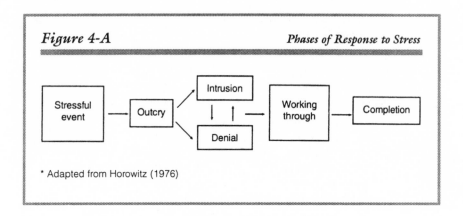

**Figure 4-A**                    *Phases of Response to Stress*

* Adapted from Horowitz (1976)

responses, but we'll first consider what happens in the wake of more serious events.

Each of the boxes in Figure 4-A represents a state of mind characterized by particular emotional experiences, cognitions, and symptoms.

The first phase is *outcry*. In a sense, a state of outcry is simultaneously an eruption of intense, unpleasant emotion (sadness, fear, and so on) *and* denial ("I *can't* believe it. It *can't* be true"). The person is in a state of shock and may be engulfed by very strong emotions. This phase of the reaction can last for just a few minutes, a few hours, or a few days. Rather quickly, the person moves into phase two, which may be either a state of *intrusion* or a state of *denial.*

*Intrusion* occurs when a person experiences waves of intense emotion and a strong impulse to think about, imagine, remember, or mentally relive the stressful event. These experiences are deemed as "intrusive" because generally the strong feelings and repetitive thoughts are not brought on willfully. The person does not choose to feel or remember; it just happens.

### Case Example:   Dale

Following the accident, Dale had to identify his wife's body. In the two weeks following her death and during periods of "intrusion," he would continue to imagine seeing her at the morgue. He would have extremely vivid memories of looking down at her body and then being overwhelmed by horror and grief. Dale said, "I know it sounds morbid, but I keep thinking about it over and over again. Sometimes I can't help it, the memories just come into my mind. Sometimes I kind of want to think about it or need to think about it." Dale thought this impulse or need to remember sounded "sick" and "morbid," although this is a very common and natural experience for many people who have witnessed something horrifying or who have experienced a tragic loss.

During a state of intrusion, emotions feel very raw, people feel extremely vulnerable, easily overwhelmed, and close to tears; they startle easily, don't sleep well, and often have nightmares. In these times, a familiar song or a fragrance can trigger a surge of sadness or anxiety. Ordinary defenses are compromised, and it is as if the mind is in direct contact with the full force of the painful feelings and realities. People don't choose to be in this place; they find themselves there automatically.

Most high-functioning, mentally healthy individuals living through a period of intrusion will experience very strong emotions. Such emotional intensity may be unfamiliar and very frightening, but generally these intense emotions do not lead to severe emotional dyscontrol. The intense affect can be tolerated.

Phase two also includes a state of *denial.* Denial may occur directly following outcry or may come on the heels of a period of intrusion. As noted earlier, denial is a state of emotional numbness. People often feel nothing. Psychic numbing takes many forms: denial (e.g., denying the significance of an event: "Well, it's not that bad. I'll get over it"); emotional blunting or numbing (a conscious awareness of the stressful events, but an inner sense of deadness, emptiness, absence of emotion); withdrawal (withdrawing from work, from friends, from life in general); and sometimes a peculiar sense of confusion, disorientation, fuzzy thinking, and feelings of unreality (dissociation and derealization).

---

**Case Example: Dale**

Dale also reported these experiences when Joyce died. "For two weeks I was an emotional basket case. Then suddenly I felt nothing. Like somebody pulled the plug. I kind of felt like I was on drugs. I was sleepy and lethargic. I started feeling guilty. I loved my wife so much, how come I can't even feel anything for her now? I can't even cry." This period of numbness lasted about six weeks and was followed by yet another wave of intrusive pain.

---

In the weeks or months following severely stressful events people will typically go back and forth between periods of denial and intrusion. Each state of mind may last for a few days or even for a few months, and then the shift occurs. Many people think that they are "over it," having lived in a state of denial and numbness for a number of weeks, only to be surprised when suddenly they are hit by a new wave of grief or distressing memories. Friends and relatives may begin to believe that a widow is coping well with her loss, and yet a month later wonder why she is so upset and easily brought to tears. This alternation may be hard for the person or friends and relatives to understand. However, such responses may not be entirely random. There appears to be a pattern to these ebbs and flows of emotion. Let's consider the possibility that the human mind somehow inherently knows that *painful realities must be faced* and that difficult emotions must be experienced, but people cannot cope with these demands all at once. Thus what is seen is a gradual process, a pacing, a rhythmic shifting back and forth between pain and psychic anesthesia. Facing the full intensity of painful realities can be traumatic. So it appears that automatic checks and balances exist in the human mind that push toward awareness and feeling, and then periodically retreat into numbness. This process is not conscious; it is more or less automatic.

If this vacillating rhythm of pain and anesthesia continues long enough, the intensity of emotional intrusion starts to lessen. Usually the pain does not completely stop, but the volume is turned down, bit by bit. Repeatedly experiencing the thoughts, memories, images, and feelings surrounding painful events in a process of desensitization, over time, drains away some of the more intensely distressing emotions. People come to face more directly the painful realities, and gradually the accompanying emotional intensity decreases.

> *Those creatures who find everyday experience a*
> *muddled jumble of events with no predictability, no*
> *regularity, are in grave peril. The universe belongs to*
> *those who, at least to some degree, have figured it out...*
> — Carl Sagan, *Broca's Brain*

Many people coping with the impact of severe stressors misunderstand the vacillation in emotional states seen in the stress response syndrome; many conclude that it is a manifestation of mental illness or emotional instability. When these emotional responses occur in healthy individuals, it is important for the client and therapist both to recognize them for what they are; that is, aspects of a naturally occurring and healthy psychological process. Just as bleeding and clot formation are aspects of physical healing, the oscillation between intrusion (awareness and feeling) and numbing are important phases of emotional healing. It is important to help clients understand this and, at the same time, to respect the process — to know when someone is in the healing process and to appreciate and accept it.

Elements of the stress response syndrome are also seen in situations where the stressors are neither abrupt nor intense.

---

**Case Example:  Sharon**

Sharon has recently become more and more aware of her sense of aloneness and of the emptiness in her marriage. The problems in her marriage did not develop overnight, so, in a sense, the stressful "event" in her life is not sudden. But it is intense.

These issues mean a lot to her, and her feelings have become stronger in recent times because her awareness of her problem has increased. Sharon also moves back and forth between times of tearfulness and despair and times when she feels better, less hopeless, and kind of numb. From time to time when she is feeling especially bad, she will mention her concern to her husband, Tim. On several occasions, he's said to her, "I thought you were over that. We've talked about this a hundred times before. I thought you were better now. Why the hell are you letting this get to you again?!" Her "pain," her dissatisfaction and loneliness, did not really go away or get better, but she did enter a state of partial denial in which the intensity of her emotions lessened. During these times, she would think "Oh, I'm OK. I'm just making a big deal out of nothing." But she was not OK. The real concerns, the real pain was simply in temporary hibernation.

---

Intrusion and denial do not necessarily alternate in a predictable cycle. Sometimes the predominant state of mind is one of intrusion. There may be a relative absence of denial. In this situation, a person seems chronically plagued with repetitive thoughts (e.g., repeated images or ruminations regarding something bad that has happened) or worries about the future.

Following painful life events, many people go through the aforementioned states of intrusion and denial over and over again (a process often referred to as *working through*), and sooner or later, the intensity of grief, fear, and so on begins to wane. It is not time that heals, but the effect of repeated exposure to reality and strong inner feelings that makes a difference. (We'll discuss more about this idea shortly.) Many people navigate these waters fairly well; they suffer, they struggle, but they heal.

What is meant by the term *completion?* This term does not have exactly the same meaning implied by the familiar phrase, "getting over it." Major life events that cause intense emotional pain, in some respects, may stay with people for a lifetime. Ask any person who has been raped, has lost a child, or has gone through a traumatic divorce, "Are you completely over it?" Even years and years after the experience, the typical answer is, "No. Not completely." These tragic, painful events matter a lot to people. It makes sense that very major events have lasting effects. However, thankfully, with time and emotional healing, changes do occur. The anguish decreases in frequency and intensity, new realities come to the forefront of life, and the memory of the painful event slips into the background. Finally, at some point, people start to feel "normal" again. Some painful memories are still there, but life gets back on track.

In people who are mentally mature and exhibit good ego strength, movement through the various states of the stress response syndrome occurs in a fairly natural and automatic way. At the heart of this process is repeated reality testing and a type of desensitization, with repeated exposure to painful emotions and memories, the affective charge attached to painful events often diminishes. Also, it is likely that completion or resolution is accompanied by a sense of mastery, for example, "This bad thing happened, it was tremendously painful, but I have faced it and survived. I can now remember it and the memory has lost the power to overwhelm." The restoration of some sense of emotional control and mastery (versus powerlessness) is a critical variable in psychological healing.

Let us consider the elements of the stress response syndrome to embody the more *automatic* aspects of emotional healing. People do not consciously choose or will this; it happens naturally. Beyond this, however, are four major *actions* that emotionally healthy people often employ, which appear to be essential ingredients in emotional healing. We examine those actions in the next chapter.

## *Summary*

- Certain symptoms and complaints can best be understood not as pathology, but as manifestations of natural, human experiences that are an integral part of emotional healing.

- A good deal of the literature on psychotherapy focuses on pathology. Psychotherapists must also have a working model of mental health and emotional healing; that is, understanding fundamental aspects of psychological healing and growth.

# Actions That Facilitate Emotional Healing

Although the concept of "working through" originally was proposed by psychoanalysts, the process has been widely embraced by a number of schools of psychotherapy. This important, but somewhat vague, concept has also found its way into everyday language; in that context it seems to mean getting through hard times or getting over an emotional crisis. But what does "working through" really mean, when it comes to emotional healing?

It's important to note that "working through" is not the same as "getting over it" or "going around it." The emphasis is clearly on both words: *Working* implying effort, action, or will, and *through* inevitably involves a passage through the reality of personal meanings and painful feelings.

Psychologist Stephen Johnson has a shorthand prescription for the process of working through: "Claim it, name it, aim it and tame it" (1985). "Claiming it" means to notice, acknowledge, feel, express, and own a feeling. "Naming it" means to put words to it, to understand it, to find meaning in the feeling. "Aiming it" is to make connections, to understand where the feeling comes from. And "taming it" means eventually to get to the point where the intensity starts to diminish. The diminished emotional suffering he refers to does not mean blocking out pain or psychologically gritting teeth, but that at some point, the person is able to talk openly and honestly about painful events, and the emotions are bearable. While the human psyche will naturally enter the various phases of the stress response syndrome, working through is a process that people actively *choose* to promote healing. The decision and courage to go through this process willfully can occur with a friend, relative, or therapist.

Let's take a look at the four key elements seen in this working-through process.

❖ *Emotional Expression*

> *When such as I cast out remorse*
> *So great a sweetness flows into the breast.*
> — W. B. Yeats

In the 1880s Sigmund Freud and his colleague Joseph Breuer began to develop a revolutionary new treatment for emotional disorders, which would eventually evolve into what is now called psychoanalysis. One of Freud and Breuer's early discoveries was that encouraging their patients to recall vividly and talk about painful events would often lead to the expression of very strong emotions. Following sessions in which strong emotions were released, patients often noticed the lessening of or disappearance of psychological symptoms such as phobias, tension, insomnia, depression, and so forth.

One of Breuer's well-known patients, Anna O., described the approach as "the talking cure" and likened it to chimney sweeping, because after a session she felt somehow cleansed. This particular approach has subsequently been called *abreaction* or *catharsis*. Catharsis is not just a technique of psychotherapy, however. In many societies across the globe, cultural rituals are designed to help bring people in close contact with their inner feelings, particularly common in many forms of bereavement ritual. Evoking strong emotions occurs in the healing practices of shamans, faith healers, and witch doctors. In Western societies, people give permission and support to others to grieve openly after the loss of a loved one. Etched into global human wisdom is some awareness of the value of outwardly expressing painful feelings. Release of strong feelings, especially by crying, helps to discharge tension, and there is some speculation that affective expression may be accompanied by changes in neurochemistry (possibly leading to the sense of relief that many people experience after a "good cry")(Frey, 1983). Expressing feelings involves not only a physical expression of emotion, but also a change in perception of emotions; it facilitates noticing, acknowledging, and admitting to these inner experiences.

Whether or not catharsis is experienced as helpful depends on a number of factors. First and foremost, can the strong emotions be endured? As we will explore in detail in later chapters, for many people (especially those with severe personality disorders or post-traumatic stress disorders) intense affective arousal may be experienced as overwhelmingly intense, and operate to derail rather than to promote healing. Thus, one's level of ego functioning and current capacity for affect-tolerance are significant in determining whether catharsis is helpful or harmful.

Second, the emotional expression must be done in an interpersonal context in which there is non-judgemental support, to reduce the likelihood that the person will feel embarrassed or ashamed.

Finally, catharsis, in and of itself, may not be the critical element in working through. What seems crucial is to *make sense out of and find meaning in the experience,* not just to feel it. The best way to accomplish this is for people to talk about what's going through their minds while experiencing strong emotions, to articulate the memories, the thoughts, and the images that accompany feelings. In the words of Kansas psychologist Mary Jo Peebles, "Words carve out coherence from a blur of feelings."

## ❖ *Talking*

> *Give sorrow words.*
> *Silence whispers the or' fraught heart*
> *And bids it break.*
> — William Shakespeare

When Anna O. called it the "talking cure," not the catharsis cure, she was onto something. Often people say, "Oh, talking about it won't help," or, "How can *just* talking help?" or, "I've talked about it a lot; it hasn't helped!" How *can* talking help?

First it is important to note that clearly some types of talking don't help at all. Certain kinds of talk intensify misery in a powerful way. In listening to clients we often hear inaccurate conclusions, critical or negative self-labeling, and unrealistic "shoulds." This type of talking does not lead to healing. It increases suffering. Examples may include:

*"What the hell is wrong with me?! I'm just screwed up!"*
*"I can't do anything right. I am a complete failure"* (overgeneralized conclusion)
*"I'll never get over this depression"* (negative prediction)
*"I should be ashamed of myself."*

Many kinds of talk also operate in the service of defense, taking people far away from experiencing inner emotions. In such cases language can help avoid or distort truth. Let's look at several examples.

- *Quick Closure*
  *"Yes, I know it's bad, but I'll get over it."*
  (then changing the subject)

- *Minimizing*
  *"Oh, it's not that bad."*
  *"Well, other people have gone through worse things. I shouldn't complain."*
  *"I feel sad, but I'm OK. I can handle it."*

- *Injunctions*
  *"I need to be strong."*
  *"I shouldn't cry."*
  *"I can't get emotional. I've got to get myself under control."*

- *Outright Denial*
  *"I'm not upset. I'm OK."* (choking back the tears)

In each of these cases, the words (or thoughts, if not spoken aloud) direct the focus away from inner emotions or the awareness of painful realities. Sometimes this process is temporarily helpful, especially when a person is feeling very overwhelmed. These natural human maneuvers are designed to protect people from too much pain. But all forms of defense can, at times, backfire and result in excessive blocking of honest emotions.

In a very different way, some forms of talk can open doors to inner feelings and promote emotional healing. This seems especially helpful if people can allow themselves to talk about painful life experiences in great detail. For this type of talking to be helpful, it cannot be rushed or forced. The person needs permission to imagine and recall vividly, and then to put any thoughts, feelings, and memories into words at his or her own pace.

There are a number of reasons that this apparently simple type of talking can help. Often during times of emotional crisis, people are beset by a wash of vague, ill-defined, but disturbing emotions and sensations. Many people feel confused and unclear about their inner experiences during these times. They may notice only an intense uneasiness or tension in their bodies, a lump in their throats, or a tightness in their stomachs. They may feel a confusing array of mixed emotions, and this state of inner emotional confusion and ambiguity intensifies their sense of anxiety, uncertainty, and helplessness.

When people are able to gradually talk about inner thoughts, feelings and experiences — a process of progressive articulation — bit by bit the inner experiences often start making sense. Language can be a medium through which experience can be structured and meaning can become encoded. Vague feelings can become increasingly clear. The person makes connections between the events and feelings, as if shining a light into a dark cellar and gradually seeing more clearly what is inside. Because most people experience a greater sense of anxiety when feeling uncertain and confused, the increased clarity and understanding leaves them feeling a greater sense of mastery and control. To "come to terms with" a situation literally means to put words to the experience. Talking may be able to give coherence to vague feelings and helps people better understand inner emotions.

A small sample of dialog from one of Sharon's therapy sessions illustrates this process.

---

Sharon: *Today at work for no reason, I started crying. It was crazy. Nothing bad happened. What's wrong with me?*

Therapist: *Well, let's look at what was happening today. What went on in the office?*

Sharon: *Nothing really.*

Therapist: *Well, maybe not, but just start talking. Tell me about today.*

Sharon: *I was at work. My girlfriend Diane was talking about her love relationship and how it wasn't working out. She's talked about it before, but all of a sudden, I just started feeling terrible. I felt like I was going to cry. I don't really care that much about her love life.*

Therapist: *You said her love relationship wasn't working out.*

Sharon: *Yeah. (She looks sad.)*

Therapist: *I wonder if there was something about your conversation with her that struck a chord with you. Tell me what comes to your mind.*

Sharon: *I guess I thought, "Yeah, I know how you feel... things never work out for me either. I'm married and I'm unhappy." (She starts to cry.)*

Therapist: *That hurts. Do your tears make sense to you?*

Sharon: *Yes.*

---

In a brief interchange about the events of the day, the *meaning* and *source* of Sharon's pain became clear to her. In the vignette, her therapist adopted an attitude that incorporated the following features, "Let's see what's happened. I bet we can make sense of this." Good listeners, not just psychotherapists, do this naturally.

On close inspection, we see that Sharon showed a bit of reluctance to speak openly about the details of the events:

Therapist: *Can you tell me what went on in the office?*
Sharon: *Nothing really.*

This is an example of resistance. The therapist however, encouraged her, and she started to talk (in particular, to spell out details and not to settle for global or oversimplistic conclusions). This encouragement to talk, to recall and articulate the specifics, and to look more carefully at her experience, brought Sharon more in touch with her true self. Her sadness and confusion were replaced with greater understanding. As she became more aware of her own emotional turmoil, her feelings of sadness became an important issue to explore. It is one thing to feel sad and in a vague way to feel confused; it is quite another to feel sadness and to understand its source. Thus, talking aloud about feelings and events helps open up emotional doors, helps people get in closer touch with true inner feelings, helps them to understand themselves better, and helps them view past and current realities more clearly.

Another value in repeatedly talking about stressful events is the following: All people develop a view of the world made up of many elements that give structure and familiarity to everyday life. This view is made up of familiar places (home, work, school); it is populated with familiar people, and it is supported by a number of basic assumptions about the world (e.g., I know where my next meal is coming from, I can go to doctors if I get sick, I feel competent to take care of myself, my world is relatively safe, honesty is the best policy, and so forth).

These familiar images, people and beliefs provide sameness, stability, and support for everyday living. They help people feel more solid and grounded as they move through each day. Major stressful life events, however, alter these familiar sources of support. The loss of a job, the death of a loved one, the breakup of a marriage, or a physical assault can dramatically erode these fundamental aspects of everyday reality. Life isn't the same after people experience major stresses. The ordinary, familiar realities that provided support are now shaken up or taken away. In addition to feelings of loss, fear, and/or vulnerability, major stressors also tend to destabilize people. In most cases, the result is a sense of fragmentation, anxiety, and uneasiness (Horowitz, 1976; Janoff-Bulman, 1992).

By repeatedly talking about the stressful events (e.g., a divorce) in a context of understanding, one may gradually piece together two views of reality: "how it was" and "how it is now." Often people are tempted to try to do this quickly. Some people may think, "I know we've gotten a divorce. I see that clearly. I don't need to talk about it." Yet getting a divorce, being raped, or losing a child is not a simple event. These are extremely powerful experiences that send ripples of change into many parts of a person's life. Coming to a deep awareness of "how it is now" often takes a long time and a lot of thinking, reflecting, and talking. Many, if not most, people feel an impulse or need to talk repetitively about the painful event and their current lives, a part of the natural, repetitive urge seen in the intrusive phase of the stress response syndrome discussed earlier. Yet, many people also think, "I shouldn't belabor this. I shouldn't beat a dead horse," and quite often they think, "I shouldn't burden others with this. They'll get tired of hearing me complain." Some people may get into a pattern of nonproductive complaining, but in the aftermath of painful events, the impulse to talk about things over and over again is entirely healthy and normal.

### Case Example: Dale

I will never forget my wife or our lifetime together. At the same time, my life is different now. It's a life without Joyce. For a number of months, I couldn't or wouldn't accept it. But over and over, as if my mind kept forcing me to see reality, the idea of life without her started to sink in.

I will never choose to remember the awful details of her death, but my mind kept inflicting the memories and the images on me. And for some reason, I felt compelled to talk about the awful events in my bereavement group. I guess since everybody else in the group talked about similar experiences, I felt it was OK to do it myself. But now I know — I had to face this new reality. My life has changed and that's just the truth.

### *Other Benefits of Talking: Getting Clear About Inner Truths*

*Truth is what stands the test of experience*
— Albert Einstein

*Your vision will become clear only when you can look into your own heart. Who looks outside, dreams; who looks inside, awakes.*

— Carl Jung

Conscious views of reality are often influenced by what people have been told by others. These views may take the form of pronouncements from important others:

*"Your father is a good man"*
*"You had a perfectly normal childhood"*
*"You know, your mother really does love you"*
*"I really want to spend more time with you honey, but I have a lot of work to do"*
*"I'm doing this for your own good"*
*"Of course I love you. We're married aren't we?! I don't have to tell you I love you. You should know it!"*

Views of reality are also shaped by injunctions:

*"You shouldn't rock the boat"*
*"Don't be so sensitive"*
*"I should like my job; it does pay well"*
*"I shouldn't complain; others have it a lot worse than I do."*

These thoughts and views of reality often have a tendency to dominate conscious awareness and constitute what I call "version one" of reality. Sometimes version one may be accurate, sometimes not.

On another level is "version two," which is based more on one's own direct experience, sensations, and feelings — a type of inner truth. A common example is what may occur in the wake of a painful emotional experience: The inner reality (physical pain, hurt emotions, needs) can be ignored by using various conscious strategies, such as *rationalizing:* "Well, I'm making a big deal out of nothing. It's not that bad"; or, "I'm just too sensitive. I know I shouldn't complain"; or, "I guess it's just all in my head"; or, by using unconscious means such as *repression,* in which the feeling is partially or totally blocked out of awareness. The person may be completely unaware of his or her inner reality.

Recall Sharon's case. She initially did not even notice her anger toward Tim. She just felt upset, afraid, and tearful. For her, version one meant "Tim is a good man. He says he loves me. It could be worse. I shouldn't complain." The presence of two views of reality constitute one common form of intrapsychic conflict.

During therapy she started to listen more carefully to her inner experiences; she gradually became aware of her version two: "He is rarely at home. There is little intimacy. I feel empty, unhappy, and angry. His words say 'I love you,' but his behavior tells a different story." The old saying, "Actions speak louder than words," became true for Sharon.

Sharon's dawning awareness of the truth of her inner experience brought her in closer contact with her real self. Version one was fashioned on empty promises, words, and Sharon's own strong hopes. She wanted desperately to believe version one. But it wasn't true. As she talked and explored her feelings during psychotherapy sessions, version one began to fade and give way to version two. Tim may have had good intentions and sincerely believed that his statements of love and promises were genuine. However, the "bottom-line" reality or experience for Sharon was version two. She didn't like it, and it hurt, but it was real.

A major part of growth and emotional healing has to do with *questioning* one's own personal "version one" regarding *important others* (e.g., parents, spouses, friends, etc.); *worldviews* (e.g., "the world is fair," "bad things don't happen to good people," etc.); and *guidelines for living* ("don't be emotional," "don't be so sensitive," "don't get angry"), and *paying attention to direct experience* — inner reactions, sensations, longings, and emotions. And one of the best ways to accomplish this is to speak aloud with another, put into words inner thoughts and feelings. Speaking facilitates this important process of clarifying inner beliefs and emotions.

A passage in the Bible says, "The truth shall make you free." This phrase can have multiple meanings, and one of them applies to the process of emotional growth and healing. It's hard to define ultimate truths, but the truth being discussed here is the truth of one's self. This truth cannot be defined or dictated from without, but must be discovered from within.

*The individual in search of self-identity becomes a consumer of reality.*
— Walter Truett Anderson

When people make time to really talk about their thoughts, feelings, and other inner experiences in the process of working through, one outcome is often an increased awareness of inner truths. Revelations such as, "My childhood was not happy," "My father didn't truly express love toward me," "My job isn't gratifying," or "My mother hurt me," among many others are often the kind of discoveries that hurt and help. Our clients must then grieve the loss of illusions (e.g., the illusion of a happy childhood or a meaningful marriage). Sometimes ultimately version two is OK. A wife may start to see her husband for who he really is. Maybe that's all right, maybe not. The more accurate awareness may ignite more open conflict or problem-solving in important relationships; it may lead to the need for marital counseling or even to divorce. But for many people, the increased awareness of inner "truth" results in a decrease of internal emotional conflict and a stronger sense of self.

It must be emphasized that within each person there are usually many "truths." Most people have mixed feelings and varying opinions. So the search for "truth" is not aimed at finding "one truth," but has as its goal the discovery of any number of inner beliefs, needs, or emotions. Only when people can clarify these truths can they then begin to sort out who they are and feel more solid about the actions they choose to take.

So to recap: Talking out loud about what has happened, about inner thoughts and feelings and current realities, can be helpful in at least three ways:

- It gives coherence to vague feelings and helps people better understand inner emotions.

- It can help people to get in closer touch with true inner feelings (opening emotional doors).

- It helps people to develop an increasingly clear view of past and current realities, to become aware of inner "truths." This often reduces feelings of fragmentation, uncertainty, and anxiety, and strengthens a sense of the self.

## ❖ *Sharing the Pain*

*...in silence we would honor our private shame and make it unspeakable.*
> — Pat Conroy, *The Prince of Tides*

*The more we are willing to share, the more we connect with a common humanity in each other.*
> — John Bradshaw

*In sharing, we seek relief from our loneliness, reassurance about our worth, and release from our guilt.*
> — Sheldon Kopp

It is commonly said that shared pain is easier to bear, but it depends on how sharing is received by others. Sometimes opening up to another person makes matters worse, as in the case when the other person responds to the expression of emotion by judging. Sometimes the judging is blatant; sometimes it is subtle. Many of our clients have encountered this time and time again, and are thus understandably uneasy about revealing inner feelings. Let's look at some typical examples of judgmental comments:

- <u>*Obvious Judgment*</u>
  *"You should be ashamed of yourself."*
  *"You have no right to feel that way."*
  *"You are being too emotional, too sensitive."*

- <u>*Somewhat Disguised Judgment*</u>
  *"Gosh, you're really taking it hard, aren't you."*
  *"Now, now, don't cry."*

*"Look on the bright side."*
*"You need to put it behind you and get on with life."*

The obvious or underlying message implied is judgment: "It's wrong to feel that way," or, "There is something wrong with you." In response, the person in pain may begin to feel ashamed or inadequate, and his or her emotional expression may cease altogether. In addition, he or she is likely to become increasingly inhibited about sharing inner feelings further cutting him or her off from connection with others. In such cases, sharing is hurtful rather than healing.

Another type of nonhelpful sharing occurs when the listener quickly jumps in to offer brilliant insights or good advice. Sometimes this response is helpful, but often it is not. In fact, it generally closes the door on deeper emotional sharing.

A final type of nonhelpful sharing occurs when the listener rather quickly or in a phony, shallow way says, "I understand." True understanding is hard to achieve. People are so unique and complex in their makeup that to come even close to a state of true understanding requires a lot of listening and a good deal of time spent coming to know the other person. The friend who says, "I understand," is probably trying to be helpful and trying to express care and concern. However, the person sharing his or her pain is likely to think, "How can she really understand?" The result again is a closing down of emotions and a reluctance to share. Such experiences are bound to color the expectations of a client entering therapy, and account for initial resistances encountered as psychotherapy gets underway.

Yet, thankfully, there are good listeners in the world. Some of them have made a profession of it (healers, clergy, psychotherapists), and others are ordinary folks who are able to listen, to care, and to strive for understanding, not judgment.

Undoubtedly, many people are able to experience considerable healing and growth by keeping inner thoughts and emotions private. However, there are abundant data to suggest that both emotional and physical healing likely occur best in the context of a supportive, interpersonal relationship. Let's take a look at some of the benefits of sharing emotional pain.

When sharing pain with another person, people may experience strong but manageable emotions that otherwise would seem completely overwhelming. The other person (perhaps a psychotherapist) can serve as an anchor, providing some degree of stability and strength, thus lessening the intensity of emotional reactions.

During times of crisis, many people are flooded with a host of emotions, some of which seem either too intense or too shameful. An extremely important consequence of sharing feelings with a good listener is feeling more "OK" about having such human emotions. As the listener genuinely hears the other person and responds with compassion or understanding (rather than judgment), the person is likely to experience less guilt and shame, and even disturbing emotions often begin to seem more normal or understandable. So many people are afraid that others will be disgusted, or shocked, or critical, but a huge sense of relief can result when they reveal deep inner feelings and see that the other person hears and does not condemn. This is one important type of corrective experience that often occurs in psychotherapy.

Sharing pain with another also gives people a chance to talk out loud. We've seen the value in talking earlier, and people can and do talk to themselves, but talking is more effective when another person listens.

Finally, and very important, sharing allows people simply to be with another human being during a time of distress. Most people feel any life crisis more acutely in isolation and aloneness. Being in contact with a close friend, a loved one, or "just" a good listener can be soothing and healing. Sharing pain connects people to one another. Compassion, love, and support can play an important role in the healing process.

### ❖ *Taking Action*

Many sources of ongoing distress stem from unpleasant or toxic interactions with others. It is one thing to work from the "inside out"; that is, to deal largely with internal thoughts and emotions. It also becomes important, in order for healing to occur, that people take some form of direct action in their lives. Examples of this include being assertive with someone who is abusive or overly critical, asking for more positive time together with a loved one, restructuring one's work schedule so that it is more sane, or choosing to end a relationship that is clearly hurtful or unsatisfying.

### ❖ *Emotional Healing Under Optimal Circumstances*

We have seen that some aspects of emotional healing are set in motion in a very automatic way. On the other hand, people are also capable of engaging in certain behaviors that potentially facilitate healing and growth. One marker of mental health is the capacity for people to mobilize resources and engage in the "work" of working through. They are able and willing to face painful realities, to experience the suffering associated with difficult life circumstance; they are capable of reaching out to others for support, and know the importance of repeatedly processing experiences (by way of talking about them, reflecting, and attempting to understand the personal meanings of these painful events).

Mentally healthy people are also generally able to form relationships with other emotionally mature friends and relatives, to whom they may turn during times of emotional despair. And finally, they usually have developed good coping skills (e.g., assertiveness, communication and problem solving skills, etc.) so that they can directly intervene to alter those situations that are amenable to change.

Healthy individuals are not burdened by significant, unresolved "old wounds" and thus are better able to confront emotional challenges in stride and without exaggerated sensitivity. Likewise, during times of significant stresses, they have developed the capacity for self-soothing and an attitude of decency and compassion toward themselves.

Even with all these assets, mentally healthy people can fall prey to extraordinarily painful experiences. Bad things do happen to good people, and no one is immune to the pain of tragedy.

Most mentally healthy individuals, at times of stress or crisis, do not need psychotherapy; most are able to mobilize resources in their existing social network. However, some seek professional counseling, often because they do not want to burden others with their pain. I have had psychotherapy clients that were considerably healthier than I am. In these instances, the therapist can often provide the container for therapy to occur, encourage the person, and then sit back and watch him or her do the work of healing. These are some of the most pleasant experiences in the lives of psychotherapists!

### Summary

- An understanding of techniques and theoretical notions regarding the process of psychotherapy should be based on an appreciation of fundamental elements inherent in emotional healing.

# Emotional Growth and the Development of the Self

O ne task facing all human beings is coming to terms with and healing from significant emotionally painful experiences that inevitably occur in people's lives. On a parallel track is what many people consider to be another critical and ongoing experience: personal growth. Although this can be defined in a multitude of ways, one of the more important aspects of this developmental process can be described in terms of discovering one's "true self." Before discussing this concept, let us consider the issue of socialization and its impact on character formation and experiences of "self."

For all young people the drive to survive (both physical and emotional survival) is a fundamental aspect of the human condition. Obviously, children have no control over the kind of environment into which they are born. Whether the early family environment is growth promoting or severely emotionally damaging, the drive to survive is hardwired into all children's biology and psyches. Adaptation — the mechanism of survival — is a blend of two powerful forces: *self-expression* and *accommodation*.

## ❖ Self-Expression

*Self-expression* basically means being who you are: expressing true inner feelings, needs, thoughts, opinions, and actions. Self-expression is felt to arise spontaneously out of the "true self" — the authentic, natural expression of who people are. Self-expression can aid adaptation tremendously. For example, the infant who feels hungry cries. Crying is a natural response to an inner state of need, and many times crying serves an adaptational role; it is an action the baby makes to get a response. The parent responds by feeding the baby, which serves the goal of survival. In adulthood, self-expression also aids adaptation. If a person is being mistreated, hurt or used, to take a stand and say, "Stop treating me this way" or, "I want you to take my feelings into consideration" can be an important survival tactic, and may dramatically improve the quality of an ongoing relationship.

In addition to serving adaptational needs, self-expression is a primary source of feelings of aliveness. Many people experience times during which they feel a special zest for life, a desire to be in the world, and a sense of hope for the future. Often these kinds of feelings naturally arise when life is going your way. Such feelings are also promoted by actions that express one's true, inner self.

Often when people are able to identify their true inner feelings, beliefs, and needs, these can operate to inform decisions (e.g., choice of career or friends), which ultimately are experienced as more satisfying. We might consider these inner experiences as a sort of internal guidance system. Finally, acting from one's inner, true self can facilitate certain positive emotional states. These experiences are described in many different ways, including feeling more solid or grounded, feeling more honest or authentic, experiencing less internal (intrapsychic) conflict, and a harmony of head and heart.

❖ *Accommodation*

The second force of adaptation is accommodation: to change something about yourself so that you'll get your needs met (be loved, feel safe, etc.).

> *Too often, as children, we were encouraged to try to be something other than ourselves. It was demanded that we assume a character and live out a life-story written by someone else. The plot line was given and improvisations were seriously discouraged or completely unacceptable, and the direction was an oppressive form of close-quarter tyranny. Neurosis is, in part,*

*the result of being miscast into a scenario plotted out*
*in accord with somebody else's unfulfilled dreams*
*and unfaced anxieties.*

— Sheldon Kopp
*Blues Ain't Nothing but a Good Soul Feeling Bad*

Random behaviors that spring naturally from infants (e.g., laughing, crying, smiling) are seen as expressions of the early true self. With time, certain behaviors or ways of being emerge that parents do not like or do not tolerate. Parents communicate disapproval in many ways. Sometimes it's very explicit: scolding a child, spanking him, sending him to his room. Often, disapproval is a more subtle, but quite powerful nonverbal message to the child: a "you should be ashamed of yourself" facial expression when the child exhibits a forbidden behavior.

## Shame: The Great Inhibiting Emotion

In all cultures people teach children the ways of society by example, by encouragement, and by the use of punishment. Without this experience youngsters do not internalize society's values. With time, these messages become the inner voices of conscience that guide a child's behavior. One version of punishment seen across cultures is shaming (humiliation, ridicule, embarrassment). Shaming goes beyond normal "shoulds" and "shouldn'ts" — in its extreme forms, it gives a child a severe message: "In a basic way there is something wrong with you. You disgust me." At the emotional core of this message are two critical elements: (1) an attack on the basic worth of the child, and (2) an implicit communication, "Shape up or get out of my sight." The implied threat is abandonment.

Shaming is a powerful emotional experience that shapes and molds the child's emerging personality, inhibiting honest self-expression. It can be an ongoing source of despair.

Parents' obvious or subtle messages of disapproval touch on the child's strong inner need to be loved and to feel safe. So, typically, most children accommodate by altering their behavior. As many parents can attest, the effects of this accommodation may be temporary, or they may be profoundly long lasting. When the latter is the case, the child may completely block out an entire aspect of his or her being. Indeed, this type of accommodating often lasts a lifetime as an aspect of character.

----

**Sharon**

I'd sometimes go and sit by my Dad's feet and look up at him. He'd be reading the paper, and then he'd just look down at me with this look on his face that said, "Well, what do you want?" He seemed annoyed, impatient. I'd just walk away. At some point I guess I just stopped going in to be with him.

----

Let's consider a metaphor, the "house of the self." In this illustration, the child begins life as an authentic albeit immature and underdeveloped self. All felt needs, emotions, and behaviors are spontaneous, unencumbered by social pressures to behave in a certain way. The initial blueprint of this new house of the self shows a small structure, but one with great potential for adding on new rooms and for remodeling, as the child grows and has new experiences.

Let's further develop this metaphor by looking at a concrete example, Carl. His early house has a number of "rooms" — one for cute and endearing behaviors, which arise spontaneously and evoke positive responses from his parents. He has some fairly neutral rooms, which he can enter and are evident as he plays quietly with a toy or looks out the window into his backyard, just taking in the scenery. And there is also a room of frustration and irritability, which he enters when he is tired, hungry, uncomfortable, and cranky. Now, let's track the development of his self over the years of childhood.

As a young child, Carl grew up in a home where his father reacted to Carl's expressions of anger, or even his strong voicing of opinions, with explosive abuse. As a young child, in order to survive emotionally, Carl took this entire part of himself (i.e., the natural human impulse to feel and express anger and to express opinions) and locked it away. With time these aspects of self became subject to massive repression and inhibition. At some point, not only did he not express anger; he didn't even feel it. He cut off a part of his true self and locked it away.

In a sense, he has relegated this aspect of being to a closed-off room. For some people this is done to an extent such that they may certainly *feel* inner anger, but consciously suppress the urge to show it outwardly, in order to avoid rebuke. When, on occasion, angry feelings are provoked and leak out into outward behavior, the person may experience a wave of anxiety (fearing rejection or counterattack) or guilt. Defenses rapidly stifle the underlying emotion and the door to the room is shut again, and avoided. For others, like Carl, the price paid for expressions of anger in his family of origin were so severe as to warrant extra efforts to banish the experience of anger even from his conscious awareness. Thus, as an adult, when confronted by events that might naturally provoke anger or an assertive response, the door is so tightly locked and sealed to that room of the self, that Carl feels no anger. Under these circumstances he is likely to experience only a vague sense of uneasiness and an inner tension, while being very cut off from his truer inner feelings. Furthermore, he may become motivated to get as much distance from the room as possible and this may be done by acting toward others in a passive, submissive, ingratiating way, as if to say, "I'm not the least bit angry. In fact you are completely right and I am wrong. Please accept my apology." This is the interpersonal behavior that compliments internal defenses against awareness of underlying emotions.

This type of accommodation and constriction of the self usually begins very early in life. It is generally not a conscious choice. Almost always a person blocks the true self to avoid emotional or physical pain. In a very real sense, this avoidance is a desperate attempt to feel love and maintain a sense of security and safety in the early home environment. Carl has paid a price for this accommodation, however; he is very passive and nonassertive. People take advantage of him. He doesn't know how to take a stand for himself. To call serious passivity "neurotic" is certainly accurate, but it's not solely pathological. When you know the context, such passivity can also be appreciated as an act of emotional survival. We might consider that within Carl as a little boy was an inner guide or compassionate protector — a part of his mind with one goal: "I am here to protect this boy, no matter what." That inner guide continues to be present, maintaining safety and protecting Carl. Significant constriction of the self is one type of adaptation that can lead to serious negative consequences. However, it is very important to appreciate that it is also fundamentally adaptive (at least in the context of Carl's early family environment).

The process of accommodation is an absolutely necessary part of growing up. It's the way all people learn to be socialized, civilized human beings. Just how much people accommodate, however, does make a difference. The process itself is not inherently adaptive nor maladaptive. But the price of socialization to some extent is always an inhibition of the true self.

Accommodation and socialization are all a matter of levels or degrees, as may be seen on the continuum in Figure 6-A.

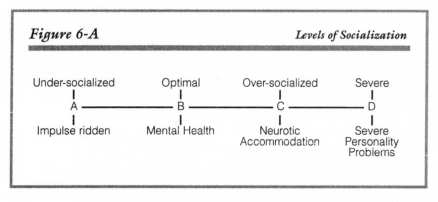

*Figure 6-A*                              *Levels of Socialization*

| Under-socialized | Optimal | Over-socialized | Severe |
|---|---|---|---|
| A | B | C | D |
| Impulse ridden | Mental Health | Neurotic Accommodation | Severe Personality Problems |

People who have rarely been required to alter their behavior are at great risk for entering life situations without internal controls over their actions. They freely act out all their feelings and desires (they are "under-socialized," or "impulse ridden.") These people exhibit blatant disregard for others and constantly violate social values. Those who have experienced extreme undersocialization are generally seen as profoundly egocentric, and often are diagnosed as narcissistic or antisocial personalities.

At the other extreme, many people are subjected to experiences of oversocialization. As constriction of the personality becomes more pervasive and severe, (in Figure 6-A, moving from A toward D), people start losing track of their true selves. The self that is out in the open for the world to see and for the individual to experience has been reshaped by compliance with the demands of others. The child has gone to such extremes to comply and accommodate that the majority of what he or she experiences or identifies as "self" may be quite different from his or her true inner self. This compliant self may properly be called a "false self" (Winnicott, 1958).

Many human experiences can be blocked out of awareness. All the basic needs can be denied. The daredevil thinks, "I don't need to feel safe; I can laugh in the face of danger." The aloof, detached person believes, "I don't need love. I don't need others." The anorexic thinks, "I don't need to eat." People can lose touch with their anger, their sexuality, their creativity, their need to be dependent and seek nurturance, their desire to be the center of attention, their need to grieve or to seek out intimacy.

Most people inhibit the true expression of self to a degree. One man may be passive and compliant at work, but he finds an outlet for power and aggression on the racquetball court. Another person is distant and closemouthed, except with a special, trusted friend, while many people feel only a whisper from within, a faint inner awareness of some feeling or need (such as sadness or love). In the extreme, some have had to massively cut off and inhibit their true selves. Their "self" feels phony and superficial, a hollow persona or fraudulent facade. This feeling is most often seen in individuals who have endured intensely critical or traumatic experiences early in life. Many people seek out psychotherapy, presenting with vague complaint, such as "life seems meaningless" or "I feel anxious and depressed, but for no particular reason." Often they are describing their own experience of being cut off from the inner self (the real potential source of aliveness).

## The Consequences of Excessive Constriction of the Self
❖ ▬▬▬▬▬▬▬▬▬▬▬▬▬▬▬▬▬▬▬▬▬▬▬▬▬▬▬▬

Inhibition and constriction of the true self can also result in an impaired ability to heal from painful life events. An analogy with the human body may serve as a metaphor. A number of important bodily systems operate to promote survival and to aid in the process of healing following disease or trauma. The nervous system can rapidly perceive danger in the environment and immediately elicit the "fight or flight" response, a complex hormonal and neurochemical reaction that mobilizes the body to take action. This action is designed either to remove a person from danger (flight) or to directly alter the situation (e.g., put out a fire, kill an attacking bear, or tell your spouse to stop criticizing you).

On a different level, the immune system has specially developed, complex mechanisms for detecting the presence of foreign organisms (e.g., viruses or bacteria) or mutant cells (as in cancer). After recognizing invading organisms, the cells of the immune system orchestrate a multilevel attack to destroy the infectious agents. Other bodily processes simultaneously aid healing by the development of blood clots, scar tissue, and so on. Thus, a number of different biological systems cooperate to fight disease and to promote healing. When the immune system is suppressed or shut down (as in the case in AIDS or other immune disorders), the natural capacity to heal becomes seriously impaired.

Likewise, as we discussed in Chapters 4 and 5, certain natural emotional healing processes and mechanisms exist within the human psyche. These healing systems naturally emerge during the course of healthy emotional development. They are aspects of the human personality and can be seen as characteristics of the true self. In positive, supportive, growth-promoting environments, such characteristics are felt to emerge spontaneously. However, adverse life experiences can interfere with the development of these emotional processes. Most people, in the course of growing up, will cut off or inhibit parts of the self — blocking off or locking away otherwise useful and adaptive abilities. Some aspects of the true self are especially designed to promote emotional healing. If these parts of the self are unavailable, the person will experience significant difficulties when encountering painful life experiences. Inhibition of healing may be the result. Let's consider some examples.

Following a major loss such as the death of a loved one or a divorce, the normal human response is to experience grief. Central aspects of grieving include the ability to talk about the one you have lost, to face painful realities, to feel the emotion of sadness, and to cry. Yet, many people have learned early in life that they should not cry. For them, crying is considered to be a sign of weakness or inadequacy.

Allowing the tears to come may be accompanied by feelings of shame or embarrassment. For other people, crying represents vulnerability (a threat to personal safety), and sadness evokes feelings of anxiety and fear. In such cases, people may grit their teeth and fight back the emotions. In more pronounced cases, the parts of the self that naturally would respond with sadness have become so stifled and cut off, that the person is totally unaware of any sad feelings at all. This individual feels nothing but a sense of numbness. In such cases, an emotional loss is not resolved and like any unhealed wound, may continue to be a source of tremendous emotional pain for many years to come.

A second example of the inhibition of healing is seen with Carl, the passive and nonassertive man. He endures ongoing problems in relationships in which some people continue to hurt and take advantage of him. The part of his self that is cut off is that natural human urge to express anger or to voice protest when he is being hurt, but it is stifled. Carl may continue to be the victim of others for a lifetime because of his difficulties in asserting himself.

Everyone wants to be accepted and valued. To meet those needs, most people accommodate and inhibit parts of their true selves. If this constriction of the self is severe, people lose touch with sources of aliveness and the natural capacities for emotional healing and growth. A central aspect of psychotherapy with many clients, thus, is determining which aspects of the self have been sealed off, and then choosing interventions that are designed to unlock those doors (to discover one's inner self and to provide encouragement, acceptance, and support for emerging self-expression). Attaining access to and encouraging development of such aspects of the self is often a central focus in psychotherapy.

All people must come to terms with three essential challenges in life: *coping* during times of stress, *healing* in the wake of painful events, and an ongoing movement toward *growth and actualization* of the self. Faced with these tasks, people must tap into internal resources, take action, and turn to others for support. However, it is clear all people are not created equal. Human beings differ considerably with regard to unique sets of assets and shortcomings.

In the next chapter, we'll consider some fundamental notions regarding mental health, and in chapters that follow, we will begin to explore, in detail, a host of common problems and psychological liabilities.

 ### *Summary*

- Excessive constriction of the true self can lead not only to a sense of emotional deadness and lack of vitality, but can also play a major role in inhibiting a number of critical psychological processes that are essential to growth and emotional healing.

# Characteristics of Mental Health

To navigate through difficult times and continue along the path of ongoing personal growth, certain personality characteristics appear to facilitate these processes significantly. An assumption adopted by many psychology writers is that optimal mental health is most likely to emerge in the context of three interactive factors: nature, nurture, and fate. *Adequate physical health, freedom from disease or biological handicaps, an intact nervous system,* and *a positive temperamental endowment* together establish the foundation for optimal emotional development. "Good enough" early experiences of nurturance, attachment, encouragement, challenge, and support are considered key ingredients in fostering sound personality development. And good luck plays a role as well. Clearly children who grow up unencumbered by severe poverty, crowded living conditions, dangerous environments, and tragic losses have a significant leg up on less fortunate kids. The confluence of these three factors weighs heavily on eventual developmental outcomes with regard to ego formation, the acquisition of social and other competency skills, and the emergence of "self."

In later chapters we look at a host of personality liabilities. In this chapter, let's lay out the characteristics that appear to be essential for mental wellness. One of the most useful such lists has been suggested by James Masterson (1986). Let's examine his list of seven characteristics:

1. *Spontaneity and Aliveness of Affect.* This characteristic reflects the ability to experience the

full range of human emotions and to feel these
emotions deeply.

2. *The Ability to Identify Inner Feelings, Wishes, Needs,
   and Thoughts.* This ability is more than just
   noticing inner experiences; it involves the capacity
   for understanding of one's feelings, needs, and so
   on, to attach some meaning to these inner
   experiences. For example, a person who has been
   recently divorced notices his inner sense of
   loneliness and says to himself, "I feel sad and alone.
   It's not pleasant. I long for companionship." His
   inner experiences are not those of vague
   discomfort, but rather emotions and thoughts that
   can be understood in the context of his life. This
   capacity has also been referred to as *psychological
   mindedness.*

3. *Self-Entitlement.* A person has an internalized sense
   that "it is OK for me to feel good about myself
   when I accomplish things. I am entitled to have
   feelings of pride and to value what I do." This
   inner permission to feel good about oneself is
   probably an outgrowth of having had early
   experiences with parents who provided support and
   praise, not only for accomplishments, but simply
   for being alive and a part of the family. A related
   characteristic is the *ability to internally generate
   feelings of worth and self-esteem.* Everyone likes to
   receive praise from others. It feels good to be
   acknowledged or to get a pat on the back.
   However, the psychologically mature person is not
   constantly in desperate need of affirmation from
   the outside. He or she can often draw on his or her
   own inner sources of self-worth.

4. *Self-Assertion (or Self-Activation).* This is a twofold
   process. It begins with the inner *belief* that it is OK
   to express one's personal opinions, feelings, needs,
   and so on, and to defend oneself if they are being
   hurt by others. In addition, it is the ability and
   willingness to put these inner beliefs into *action,* to
   take a stand, to voice an opinion or express oneself.
   Mature people have the capacity to act assertively

while taking the rights, needs, and feelings of others into consideration.

5. *The Ability to Provide Self-Soothing.* This very important point deserves a lengthier discussion. All people ultimately experience losses, setbacks, and personal failures — absolutely unavoidable events in life. The personal pain that results from losses and failures can be tremendous. Self-soothing, a sort of nurturing that takes place within oneself, encompasses a wide array of attitudes and behaviors.

The first step is a deep, inner belief, an attitude of compassion toward oneself: "I am hurting and I have a *right* to do something to ease my pain." Many people of course, do not feel OK about this basic human right. They may think that they deserve to feel awful or think, "I'm just feeling sorry for myself." This attitude often reflects their early experiences of unsuccessfully seeking comfort from others. Many children are told directly to stop being "cry-babies," to stop feeling sorry for themselves. The parental injunction is that it's not OK to acknowledge hurt and especially not OK to ask for comfort. The child internalizes this message, which can become a lifelong, core belief. The emotionally mature person has usually been fortunate enough to have been genuinely cared for early in life and has developed an internalized capacity for self-compassion.

Self-soothing also takes the form of remembering and calling forth positive images of past successes or love. For example, Susan just experienced a very painful rejection. Paul, who she had been dating, told her that he was fed up with her and had, in fact, been seeing another woman for the past month. He said to Susan, "You are a loser. I should have left you a long time ago." In the midst of her sadness and hurt, Susan often tells herself that she isn't a loser. She reminds herself of the many good friendships in which she has been valued and loved, and she remembers a number of occasions when she has made a difference in the lives of friends and family members. These thoughts and memories are not mere rationalizations designed to deny her hurt. Rather, they are actual facts about her and her life experiences that help her to preserve a sense of selfworth in the wake of Paul's rejection.

One of my former professors was dying of cancer. He told me that he would frequently recall his years of teaching and the numerous students whom he had taught. He recalled the many occasions in which he knew he had made a real difference in his students' lives. These memories gave him comfort and a sense of meaning as he was living through times of intense physical pain and facing the reality of impending death.

Another type of self-soothing can be seen in the willingness for people to do things to nurture themselves. This can take many forms, including taking a day off from work to rest or engage in some form of recreation; giving yourself permission to take a hot bath, to get a massage, or to buy new clothes; making a point to say "no" to others' requests and thus free up more personal time; feeling "OK" about turning to a friend to share painful emotions.

A final aspect of self-soothing is the decision to be kind to yourself and to avoid harsh self-criticism; to develop a genuine sense of selfcompassion.

Many people have not developed the ability for self-soothing; this is especially so in individuals suffering from severe personality disorders or chronic depression.

6. *Intimacy.* The capacity for intimacy involves the ability to express ourselves in an open and honest way with someone we love. This may involve the sharing of tenderness, neediness, or emotional pain.

The risks of intimacy can be potential loss and vulnerability. However, the rewards are many, including one very important resource during times of emotional pain — the relationship with another human being to whom a person may turn for comfort and support.

7. *Commitment.* This is the ability and willingness to "stick with it" during difficult times. Commitment is evident, for example, in a relationship in which the couple is going through a period of distress and frustration, yet the partners manage to stay connected and "hang in there" until the stress subsides. In part this involves the capacity for frustration tolerance and delay of gratification. But it also depends a good deal on a sense of hopefulness (hopefulness in general about interpersonal relationships and hopefulness, in particular, in the context of the specific relationship). This form of healthy commitment is not the decision to stay in a very pathological relationship for a long time. Staying in very destructive relationships can be extremely emotionally damaging. Rather, the commitment Masterson speaks of is an involvement in an important relationship in which the couple is willing to endure some degree of distress for a period of time because they have committed themselves to their relationship. Undoubtedly, this capacity to rise above emotional pain and maintain a loving connection probably reflects the influence of early life experiences. Fortunate children growing up in emotionally healthy homes have experienced at a deep level the knowledge that they will continue to receive love and not be abandoned even during difficult times.

To Masterson's list of seven crucial personality characteristics I would like to add another.

8. *Having a Profound Understanding for One's Humanness.* The concept is captured well by the writings of psychiatrist Cliff Straehley (1990):

> *By humanness, I really mean fallibility or imperfections. This is part of the fabric of life and inescapable. [I can] have understanding for myself that this is so, and not condemn or judge myself because of it. If we can indeed*

*wholeheartedly admit this to ourselves, then a
tremendous burden may be lifted from our
shoulders. The price for the removal of this burden
is humility. Paradoxically, when we are able to
admit to ourselves that we can't control everything
and only can offer life our best at the moment, it
gives us a profound permission to be ordinary.*

The eight characteristics described in this chapter are
the critical components of healthy personalities, aspects of
the self that allow people to live through painful times, to
heal, to recover, and to grow.

These characteristics may emerge naturally, given
positive experiences early in life (in terms of nature,
nurture, and fate). Certainly, attaining this favorable state
of emotional development in no way provides people with
*protection* from emotional pain. It does, however, equip
them with the basic personality characteristics that can
facilitate the processes of emotional healing and growth.
And, as we explore in later chapters, these are some of the
characteristics that a therapist may choose to foster and
strengthen in clients.

### ❖ *Summary*

- Psychotherapists must become keen observers
  of not only problems and pathology, but
  manifestations of psychological strength. These
  can serve as markers to track change over time,
  and when identified and openly acknowledged
  with our clients, can be a helpful way to provide
  support and to honor growth.

# PART TWO ❖

---

*Maps of the Mind:*
*Making Sense of Adaptation*
*and Pathology*

> ...in embarking on therapy with a particular
> patient, the journey will be greatly facilitated if
> the therapist makes use of a map...as every
> psychotherapist can testify, there is recurrent
> danger of getting lost
> — Strupp and Binder, 1984

# The Cognitive Perspective

This chapter considers several key theoretical concepts, laying the groundwork for the later chapters, which specifically address treatment.

## The Role of Cognitions in Adaptation and Psychopathology

The term "cognitive" is often misunderstood as being synonymous with "thinking." The concept is, however, much broader. Cognition actually refers to the process of "knowing," and thinking (logical, analytical thought) is but one source of information. People do depend on thought processes to glean information about life events, external circumstances, and other demands of reality. In addition, a good deal of information is derived from a multitude of sensory experiences (perceptual data from the outside world) as well as input from within. This includes physiological sensations, "gut feelings," images, hunches, memories, and intuitions.

A basic assumption adopted in this book is that it is highly adaptive to pay attention to all sorts of data regarding one's reality (both external reality as well as the reality of inner feelings, needs, urges, and sensations). Such data are essential for at least two purposes; the first is survival (both physical and social-emotional survival). Without accurate information about external events, people are at grave risk from the outside — of being run over by a bus, for example, or failing to adapt to certain social settings. Accurate reality testing is crucial for problem-solving, planning, anticipating consequences, assessing cause and effect, and modifying behavior.

Second, a window into one's interior life and self can serve adaptation. Only by having a fairly accurate awareness of one's inner feelings, needs, beliefs, and values can people make appropriate choices as they navigate through life. This may pertain to major life decisions, such as choice of career or intimate partners, or to minor day-to-day actions, such as choosing how you want to spend an evening.

People with markedly impaired sensory systems (e.g., those who are blind and deaf) face great dangers and challenges in negotiating basic safety and survival. Those with serious impairments in reality testing (e.g., severely psychotic people) are at tremendous risk for making incredibly poor judgments or behaving in ways that can at times be life-threatening. Likewise, many people are not at all clear about the inner realities of their own, unique selves, and thus move through life like a boat without a rudder. Often the price paid by those with poor internal reality testing is that they enter into life-styles, jobs, religions, and relationships that are ultimately unsatisfying and out of synch with inner, but largely unrecognized needs. Their directions in life may have been charted by others who have imposed their own script for living one's life, a direction that may or may not fit one's particular set of attributes, limitations, and needs.

A number of models of psychotherapy accept the notion that one major focus for treatment is to help clients improve reality testing (a goal that I will speak of as "getting clear"). This can apply to the perception of external events. Let's illustrate with some examples.

- Developing a more accurate perception of the realities of another person or a relationship. Becoming more clear about how one is being treated or what another person's true motives and feelings are.
- Assessing the realistic pros and cons associated with a major life decision.
- Facing the realities of a tragic life event, such as the death of a loved one.
- Realizing the truth about how someone was really treated as a child.
- Considering the realistic risks associated with a

certain behavior (e.g., the actual risks in air travel in a person with a fear of flying).
- Penetrating denial about serious substance abuse in a loved one.
- Realizing more fully the consequences of one's own reckless behavior.

In each of these cases, and numerous other situations that are the focus of psychotherapy, various techniques can be used to facilitate the process of improving reality testing and "getting clear."

Improved *internal* reality testing is also often the focus of many therapeutic interventions, as illustrated by the following examples:

- Realizing more clearly how it feels to be used or hurt by another.
- Discovering inner feelings of vulnerability or neediness (in someone who has always considered himself to be very unemotional and self-reliant).
- Determining that one desires a greater amount of closeness and intimacy in a relationship.
- Appreciating the depth of inner feelings of sadness following the loss of a close friend.
- Facing the reality of inner emotions of terror in the aftermath of being raped.

Cognitive-behavioral approaches have largely focused on isolating and correcting errors in thinking that pertain to the assessment of external realities (challenging all-or-none, categorical thinking, or reducing the tendency to jump to conclusions or make unrealistic negative predications). Conversely, the centerpiece of more psychodynamic models has been a focus on inner, subjective experiences and the importance of developing a clearer awareness of internal "truths" (both conscious and unconscious inner experiences). Yet these need not be seen as mutually exclusive processes. Let's take a closer look.

## ❖ *Information Processing*

Classical psychoanalytic theory proposed two types of thinking (information-processing styles): primary and secondary process thought. More recent theorists have expanded this to include a third major mode of thinking: experiential processing. The three cognitive styles are characterized as follows (Epstein, 1994; Greenberg et al., 1993):

1. *Conceptual Processing:* deliberate, conscious, volitional thinking that is often sequential in nature. This is what most people consider to be rational-logical thinking.
2. *Experiential Processing:* effortless, often quite an automatic sensing or knowing; most often a nonverbal mode of information processing that can be described as involving intuition, hunches, "gut feelings," images, and metaphors. Experiential processing can be conscious or can occur on the edge of awareness (preconscious) and frequently carries with it some affective valence.
3. *Primary Process Thinking:* a style of thinking and experiencing that is alogical and arational. It is often experienced as highly affectively infused images and fragmented, disorganized cognitions. As classic psychoanalytic writings described it, primary process thinking is characteristic of mental activity seen in dreams and in psychosis.

It is also helpful to subdivide experiential processing into two types. The first version is seen most commonly in situations where something has evoked a strong emotional response. I will refer to this type as *impulsive experiential processing*. In moments of intense affective arousal, people tend to process information in a crude way. Thinking is characterized as being categorical (black-and-white thinking, for example, "Is it safe or is it dangerous?"), personal (egocentric), and concrete. Such "thinking" takes place instantaneously, and is unreflective and action oriented (Epstein, 1994). This rapid perceptual processing is fundamentally adaptive as it can serve survival in moments of actual danger (if you are about to be run over by a car, it does not pay to stop and take time to analyze the nuances of the situation). What is required is a very rapid, albeit rough assessment of the situation —"safe" or "not safe" — and a resulting action (jumping out of the path of the car).

There is some neurobiological research suggesting that such crude assessments may be carried out largely on a subcortical basis (by limbic structures, the amygdala and hippocampus). These primitive brain structures then ignite emotionally driven behaviors that operate to preserve life (in fact the root words for *emotion* are "e," meaning away from, and "motion," meaning to move. On one level emotions can be seen as the force that activates behavior).

Although this style of information processing can play a critical role in survival, it is also quite prone to faulty or oversimplistic assessments of reality. As noted above, this style is "unreflective," not readily subject to more careful scrutiny or analysis. Thus, if not subsequently processed by higher levels of cognition, it is a style that is very error prone. This is seen in many, if not most, psychiatric disorders, revealed in the tendency for people to jump to unwarranted conclusions, to think in an all-or-none fashion, to anticipate unrealistic catastrophes, or to personalize experiences. Such errors in cognitive processing can relate to the perception of external realities as well as inner experiences or views of the self (e.g., "I am a totally worthless person," is an example of all-or-none thinking). These problems in information processing have been referred to by cognitive-behavioral therapists as *cognitive distortions* (Burns, 1980).

A less impulsive version of experiential processing also exists, which I will call *reflective experiential processing*. This occurs as people look to inner hunches, sensations, and intuitive feelings, and more carefully consider them (by noticing them, letting them percolate, sitting with the experience for a while, and then striving to understand or otherwise find meaning in the inner "data"). Under these circumstances, this version of experiential processing can result in important information about both external and internal realities.

If we accept the assumption that accurate reality testing is important for navigating through life, then we can consider the following: Impulsive experiential processing is useful and adaptive in truly dangerous situations, but is also quite error prone and often maladaptive in situations that are emotionally charged but not actually dangerous. (Ultimately, of course, this style of cognition is a source of considerable unnecessary emotional suffering.)

Conceptual processing and reflective experiential processing potentially are rich sources of data regarding external and personal/internal reality. Primary process thinking, in contrast, is grossly pathological and rarely serves adaptation.

One might assume that under the best of circumstances having access to both conceptual and experiential processing would be advantageous. However, for many people this is not the case, as we see in the next section.

### ❖ *Processing Bias*

Uneven access to both styles of information processing is a very commonly encountered situation that accounts for significant adaptational difficulties. Let's first look at this by considering the extreme ends of the continuum.

Individuals who perceive the world almost exclusively via conceptual processing do not have ready access to experiential data. They try to come to terms with emotional pain, or to make critical life decisions, based on logical analysis alone, largely unaware of inner emotions, urges, or needs. In the extreme these are profoundly emotionally stilted individuals, most of whom would be characterized as obsessive-compulsive personalities. However, on some level such people do respond to emotionally provocative events, but their *experience* of inner feelings is distorted. Often they may notice only vague, inner styles of uneasiness or tension, without a clue about what they are experiencing. Such people are also quite prone to somatization; the body may be expressing that which the emotional self cannot.

Profoundly cut off from inner emotions, these people are often severely impaired in their ability to work through painful life circumstances. They are also quite prone to look to internalized "scripts" to provide an understanding of how to live their lives. Such scripts often are introjected rules or "shoulds"; encoded messages from important others, learned through the years of childhood. Examples of such scripts or injunctions are listed below.

| Common Injunctions | |
| --- | --- |
| Don't be emotional | Don't be so sensitive |
| Don't cry | Don't rock the boat |
| Don't get your hopes up | Don't be childish |
| Grow up! | Don't really trust people |
| Don't get too close | Don't ask for support |
| Don't trust your feelings | Be logical |
| Don't get mad | Be perfect |
| Don't accomplish more | Don't give up |
|   than Mom or Dad | Don't brag |
| Don't feel proud of yourself | Please others |
| Don't be selfish | Don't complain |

When asked, "How do you feel?" these people either draw a blank or respond with an answer that is a direct expression of underlying shoulds. For example, when asked how he felt about the news that his wife asked him for a divorce, one constricted, obsessional man commented, "These things are distressing, but I'm sure I'll get over it." He says "These things are distressing" (referring to the divorce in a general, abstract, and detached way) rather than saying "I feel distressed." "I'm sure I will get over it" likely reflects an overlearned cliché and does not reveal anything about his own, personal suffering. One might think that the man is being *resistant* as he sidesteps the inquiry about his inner emotions. And, in a sense he is. However, we might also be able to appreciate this as a natural manifestation of his predominant information-processing style. His ability to notice and acknowledge inner sensations and feelings is simply very undeveloped. One goal of treatment with such people, as we address in later chapters, is to increase (at least a bit) their capacity to process experientially.

The opposite end of the continuum is seen in classical hysterical (or histrionic) personalities. These people are very "in touch" with experiential data; in fact they may be drowning in it. But their limitation lies in grossly underdeveloped abilities for logical, analytical thought. When confronted with emotion-provoking events, they may be flooded by intense sensations and emotions. However, lacking the skills to understand and find meaning in these experiences, they too are impaired as they attempt to cope and to heal. As we spoke about in Chapter 5, the working through of painful emotional issues appears to require a *balance* of two factors: access to and the willingness to feel and acknowledge emotions, as well as the capacity to discover meanings, (i.e., to cognitively understand the experience, which is greatly facilitated by conceptual processing and talking out loud with another person). A part of treatment with these individuals aims at enhancing their ability to engage in at least some conceptual processing.

Two additional extremes also exist. The person who operates almost exclusively via impulsive experiential processing typically presents with marked difficulties in impulse control. This is seen is cases of intense and acute stress reactions and is a dominant characterological feature of some people with severe personality disorders (low-level borderline and antisocial personality disorders). Impulsive actions, poor judgments, and intense emotional displays dominate. The ability to work through painful experiences adequately is very limited.

Finally, those operating largely by way of primary process are, of course, gravely disabled people (those suffering from psychotic disorders and/or significant neurological impairment). These clients will certainly benefit from interventions that help them to reality test (anticipate consequences, plan ahead, and the like), but first and foremost they will require interventions designed to help reduce affective arousal and aid in emotional stabilization. Psychotropic medications are almost always the treatment of choice to help reduce the grossly fragmented thinking that such people experience. (Preston, O'Neal and Talaga, 1997).

## ❖ *Processing Conflicts*

A common problem exhibited by people entering psychotherapy is that they are faced with internal psychological conflicts. Such conflicts can be experienced consciously or at a more unconscious level. Often intrapsychic conflicts can be understood as a form of cognitive dissonance, between at least two opposing forces: what I know in a logical, conceptual way, and what I know in an experiential way. An example of this would be a man who strongly adheres to a belief, "Don't rock the boat. Don't challenge authority. Try to behave yourself and be a 'good person.'" Recently he has been exposed to increasing emotional abuse by his supervisor (who ruthlessly belittles him in front of other employees). He has been gritting his teeth and enduring the remarks. On a less conscious level, however, he has a growing sense of anger and resentment, accompanied by somatic sensations including stomachaches and tension headaches.

What is his view of the situation? What does he know? What does he feel? It all depends on which source of data analysis he pays attention to (conscious, conceptual processing or experiential, "gut" perceptions). As long as he is largely unaware of the more experiential data, he will be more prone to consciously focus on the conceptual material (the injunctions to be a "good person").

In more insight-oriented approaches, a central focus in therapy is to use techniques that facilitate increased awareness of inner, subjective, and less conscious aspects of one's experiencing (see Chapters 8 and 10). One way to view this is to aim to increase the person's capacity to notice and acknowledge this other rich source of "data." One assumption is that states of internal conflict, even if out of conscious awareness, lead to dissonance and tension, and that human beings are motivated to reduce inner dysharmony and achieve a more coherent sense of internal experiences (Epstein, 1994).

As the man is helped to become aware of his inner, more affective experiences and the truth of how he feels, he also then has more information to consider. It is not a matter of conceptual processing being wrong and experiential right. Rather, once he is clearer about his various perceptions, beliefs, needs, and feelings, he may be in a much better position to make wise choices about how to react to his boss.

## ❖ *Other Sources of Internal Conflict*

Another common problem that creates inner tension and may interfere with adaptation can arise as a "struggle between the shoulds." First, consider that there may be two versions of inner "shoulds": those that represent introjected messages from important others, and those that individuals arrive at solely on their own, as a consequence of unique personal experiences. Exploring in detail a client's inner values and beliefs may bring to light an awareness of such inner conflicts. With the increased clarity of conscious awareness, people are often in a better place to identify, understand, own, and honor their own inner values and beliefs. To do so may reduce inner dissonance, while also serving to strengthen the client's sense of self and personal identity.

## ❖ *Cognitive and Perceptual Errors*

One's daily experience is full of numerous actions, interactions, events, and an infinite array of perceptions. Some of these are unremarkable; they are the mundane stuff of everyday existence. Some are especially noteworthy because they are either emotionally distressing and negative (e.g., being treated rudely or criticized) or, conversely, quite positive (e.g., receiving an unexpected public compliment). People do not attend to all experience with the same level of conscious awareness. A good deal of moment-to-moment perception is barely registered on a conscious level, as people motor throughout the day often on "automatic pilot." But some events are certainly noticed and some become the focus of attention in such a way that they may dominate a person's life for a time (by way of thinking about, anticipating, ruminating, worrying about, and reflecting on an experience).

Human beings are obviously not matter-of-fact computers or completely objective observers and recorders of reality. A number of factors play an important role in determining what is attended to and how it is understood. Let us consider three important and influential variables.

The first are *sensitizing experiences*. Three examples can illustrate this point. The woman who is pregnant for the first time eagerly awaits the birth of her child, and she now notices pictures of babies in magazines and billboards much more often than before. This meaningful event in her life has altered her perceptions. She is biased toward noticing babies. This is not something she necessarily chooses to do; it just happens. The man who recently survived a terrible traffic accident (having his car hit by a "big rig") now can't help but notice large trucks in his rear-vision mirror while driving. He is not consciously or intentionally looking for them, but he is exquisitely sensitive to perceiving them (even on the horizon) and reacting with a temporary sense of dread. A teenage girl, following a tearful breakup with her boyfriend, now notices almost any song on the radio expressing the theme of "lost love," and she responds with a lump in her throat.

In each example, there is a *perceptual bias*. An emotionally important life event has altered the automatic processes of attending, noticing, and responding to various stimuli previously unimportant, now salient.

A second factor that may influence cognitive processing is *altered brain functioning*. Certain medical illnesses (e.g., hypothyroidism), biological conditions (e.g., postpartum hormonal changes), or the use of medication (e.g., antihypertensive drugs) can result in altered neurochemical functioning in key structures in the limbic system. In certain vulnerable individuals, changes in neurotransmitter function in the amygdala and hippocampus may play an important role in altering cognitive processing. One outcome is the tendency to focus almost exclusively on awful, negative, and pessimistic aspects of life or of oneself. This predominantly negative and bleak view of reality leads to depression and feelings of hopelessness. Such neurochemical dysfunction can occur in otherwise quite mentally healthy individuals, and may lead to severe anxiety and depressive symptoms. For many individuals severe and/or prolonged stress can also ultimately disrupt normal neurochemcial functioning in the brain. Thus, what begins as a psychological reaction evolves into a disorder with both psychological and neurobiological elements. The underlying physiological changes may then begin to alter perceptions and cognitions.

Finally, significant persistent experiences early in life contribute to the development of *enduring beliefs* (schemas) regarding the world, human interactions, and views of the self. These powerful beliefs can have a profound effect on cognitive processes, and, in particular, can influence selective attention; that is, the tendency to become especially alert to certain events while being relatively unaware of other elements of experience (schemas and schema theory are explored in detail in the next chapter).

Sensitizing events, neurochemical dysfunctions, and enduring beliefs can and do often influence perceptions and cognitions in a powerful way. When this influence results in inaccurate or incomplete views of reality, then people are handicapped. They are at greater risk for misinterpreting events, for jumping to unwarranted conclusions, for inaccurately anticipating outcomes, and for maladaptive responses (e.g., overly intense emotional reactions, behavioral inhibition, and inadequate problem-solving). This becomes a major source of *unnecessary pain*.

## ❖ *Summary*

- Central to successful adaptation and survival is the ability for accurate reality testing. A primary feature of many psychological disorders is disordered or maladaptive thinking.

- The psychotherapist must be alert to disordered thinking and may choose intervention strategies that have as a goal to help clients "get clear" about both external and internal "truths."

- Human beings are capable of processing information on a number of different levels. Often multiple or parallel processing of experience leads to confusion or to internal conflict.

# 9 ❖

---

# *Schemas and Schema Theory*

> *Significant experiences of early life may never recur again, but their effects remain and leave their mark. They are registered as memories. Once registered, the effects of the past are indelible, incessant and inescapable.*
>
> *The residuals of the past do more than passively contribute their share to the present. They guide, shape, or distort the character of current events. They operate insidiously to transform new stimulus experience in line with the past.*
>
> — Theodore Millon

Schemas represent stable and enduring beliefs regarding three spheres of experiences: beliefs about oneself, what to anticipate from interactions with others, and what to expect from the world in general (see Figure 9-A). Such beliefs are felt to develop gradually over the years of childhood as people encounter a multitude of experiences with others in their family of origin (e.g., repeated experiences of being mistreated, abused, and belittled may result in a persistent belief that, "I am unlovable and I expect to be hurt by others"). Although schema formation *may* be influenced by single, very intense events (e.g., being raped may lead to a view of the world in general as being unsafe), generally it is felt that these core beliefs emerge gradually. They are a natural consequence of repeated exposure to day-to-day interactions with others. Such beliefs, set down in childhood, if unaltered by later experiences, may continue as the nucleus of one's self-concept and worldview for a lifetime.

*Figure 9-A*                                                    *Life Schemas*

|  | Positive | Negative |
|---|---|---|
| Oneself | "I am a decent person." | "I am a loser." |
| Interpersonal interactions | "Generally I can count on others to be kind towards me." | "I expect others to reject me." |
| World view | "The world is relatively safe." | "Everywhere you go, you will be taken advantage of and you'll be screwed - the world is not safe." |

Schemas can be seen to lie along a continuum: On one end are extremely rigid, maladaptive schemas and at the other end are schemas that are positive, adaptive, and malleable.

Exposure to very painful and severe psychonoxious experiences in early years is more likely to result in schemas that are both negative (pessimistic, self-condemning) and rigid. These *early maladaptive schemas* (as they are referred to by psychologist Jeffrey Young, 1994) tend to be characterized as egocentric (very self-focused and unable to view situations from another's perspective) and categorical (i.e. oversimplistic, all-or-none, black-or-white conclusions). An example is, "I see myself as profoundly defective. If others get to know me, they will recoil in disgust or reject me. There is nothing positive about me. I am destined to be alone for my whole life." Note the extremely negative conclusions about the self. This kind of schema leaves no room for any positive attributes and holds no promises for possible growth or change. In such cases, despite some positive experiences occurring later in life, the schema goes unaltered. For example, if someone were to tell this person, "You did a great job on this most recent project at work," the person may say "Thank you," but walk away thinking "They are just saying that. They probably feel pity for me and were just trying to make me feel better. I know I did a lousy job. I know I'm a loser." Such internal "self-talk" has the power to negate new experiences in a way that maintains the negative schema. It is set in "psychic concrete," and not amenable to corrective experiences. Another common situation: A person raised by an extremely harsh and critical parent seeks out a similar person as a spouse or employee or boss, thus recreating an external environment that perpetuates the rejecting experience and reinforces the schema (repetition compulsion). These are reasons that rigid, maladaptive schemas can be so enduring.

*Positive/healthy schemas* are characterized in two ways: First, they are more realistic and balanced (not categorical). Thus a person with this kind of schema may think, "I may have done a lousy job on that project, but I also know that I have done well on others. In general, I am not incompetent, I just didn't do well on this particular project." This is not a rationalization, but rather is simply the truth. Second, the more healthy schemas are those open to modification by experience; they are more malleable. Finally, the choice to seek out healthier relationships that do not repeat early toxic patterns of

| *Figure 9-B* | *Healthy and Maladaptive Schemas* |
|---|---|
| **Healthy Schemas** | **Maladaptive Schemas** |
| Flexible, malleable | Rigid |
| Realistic | *May* be unrealistic* |
| Benign or positive | Negative |
| Balanced, complex | Categorical, simplistic |
| Allow for behavioral change | Inhibit behavioral change |

*May have been realistic in the context of the experiences of early childhood. May be unrealistic in current circumstances.

interaction is both a sign of emotional health and a life choice that may ultimately foster the alteration of underlying negative schemas.

Schemas can be seen as organized around certain themes or major dynamics. In listening to clients, especially over a period of time, we often realize that their thoughts, worries, and particular areas of emotional vulnerability reflect such underlying themes. Two especially useful lists of schemas are offered by Young (1994) and by Elliott and Lassen (1998). These are listed in Figures 9-C and 9-D.

*Figure 9-C*                              *Maladaptive Schemas*

1. *Abandonment:* expecting that others will be rejecting
2. *Mistrust/Abuse:* expecting that others will hurt or abuse
3. *Emotional Deprivation:* expecting that one's desire for support will not be adequately met by others
4. *Defectiveness/Shame:* belief that one is fundamentally bad, defective, unwanted, or inferior
5. *Social Isolation/Alienation:* belief that one is destined to be isolated from others
6. *Dependence/Incompetency:* belief that one is unable to cope with everyday life demands without help from others (often accompanied by feelings of helplessness).
7. *Vulnerability to Danger:* exaggerated fear that a catastrophe could occur at any time
8. *Enmeshment/Underdeveloped Self:* excessive involvement with others at the expense of the development of a "self"
9. *Failure:* belief that one has failed or is destined to fail due to fundamental inadequacies (social, academic, intellectual, etc.)
10. *Entitlement:* Insistence that one should have whatever one wants, regardless of the cost to others
11. *Insufficient self-control:* unwillingness or inability to control impulses or feelings
12. *Subjugation:* excessive surrendering oneself to others. Often this is done to avoid retaliation or abandonment
13. *Self-sacrifice:* excessively voluntarily meeting others needs at the expense of one's own needs
14. *Approval-seeking:* expressive emphasis on gaining approval from others

—

Early Maladaptive Schemas (Young, 1994).

As noted in the last chapter, schemas can influence here-and-now cognitions in a powerful way. The prevailing theme operates to bias ongoing perceptions in a direction supporting the underlying belief. Thus expectations, predictions, conclusions, and the processing of current experiences are subject to faulty or unrealistic perceptions. Let's illustrate this by way of two clinical examples. Both are characterized by negative schemas, but in the first case, the schemas are somewhat malleable, while in the second, they are profoundly rigid.

*Figure 9-D*                                     *Manifestations of Self-Schemas*

These authors view self-schemas as centering on particular themes, each of which may manifest as a negative, maladaptive schema (N.M.S.), a schema that is deemed "positive-maladaptive" (P.M.) in which certain positive characteristics are unrealistically and pathologically emphasized, or adaptive schemas.

| THEMES | N.M.S. | P.M. | Adaptive |
|---|---|---|---|
| Acceptance: | Blameworthy | Blameless | Accepting |
| Desirability: | Undesirable | Irresistible | Desirable |
| Worthiness: | Unworthy | Entitled | Worthy |
| Adequacy: | Inadequate | Perfectionistic | Adequate |
| Assertiveness: | Acquiescent | Domineering | Assertive |
| Capability: | Dependent | Stubbornly Independent | Capable |
| Empowerment: | Powerless | Omnipotent | Empowered |
| Resilience: | Vulnerable | Invulnerable | Resilient |
| Centeredness: | Other-centered | Self-centered | Centered |
| Intimacy: | Abandonment | Avoidant | Intimate |
| Self-definition: | Undefined | Aggrandizing | Defined |
| Trust: | Distrusting | Naïve | Trusting |

Self-Schemas (Elliot and Lassen, 1998).

Jennifer was ignored by her workaholic father and largely rejected by her mother. She came to believe strongly that, "There is something wrong with me. I am defective and in a very basic way, unlovable." Yet during her childhood, from about ages 5 to 10, their next door neighbor, a kind and gentle older woman, did provide her with a considerable amount of warmth and affirmation. Jennifer periodically continues to have times of feeling unlovable, but this belief is not rigid; it is not etched in stone. She is able to remind herself of her good qualities and can recall times when she has been in positive, meaningful relationships with others. The early experience left its mark, but later relationships have modified her beliefs so that they do not dominate her life. The malleability of Jennifer's negative core beliefs probably has to do with having experienced only moderately severe neglect/rejection, while the positive effects of the relationship with her neighbor provided a buffer. In the end, her early experiences were certainly painful, but not of a magnitude considered to be traumatic.

In contrast, we have Bruce, who grew up in a home environment of pervasive harshness, brutality, and ruthless criticism. His father daily told Bruce he was worthless, evil, and a "piece of shit." Bruce's incredibly passive mother would shrink into the shadows and seem to disappear at these times, offering no protection from his tyrannical father. Bruce is now a man in his mid-forties. He is single, lonely, and chronically depressed. He interprets his inner belief, "There is something wrong with me; I am defective and in a very basic way, unlovable," as an absolute fact. He has never thought for a moment that the belief was untrue. These are rigid and unshakable negative beliefs.

It is important to note that Bruce rarely thinks about his father or his childhood. He does not consciously feel any kind of direct pain from childhood wounds. But the powerful beliefs, laid down years ago, wreak havoc in his daily life. Negative schemas influence here-and-now perceptions and expectations. Let's take a closer look at how this process continues to happen in Bruce's life.

Bruce's firm conviction that he is unlovable influences his perceptions of the world. He is quick to notice any events that confirm or even come close to confirming his beliefs. At a recent social event taking place at his office just after business hours, he entered a room full of fellow employees. For the first two minutes he was there, no one spontaneously came up to greet him. He looked around the room, but no one met his eyes. He very quickly concluded, "They don't give a damn whether I'm here or not." This perception and conclusion were very likely to have been exactly what he anticipated. At that moment, he abruptly left the party, went home, and felt lousy. He has had similar experiences numerous times before. And many more times he has been so convinced that he would be rejected or unwanted that he didn't even attend social functions.

One consequence of negative schemas is behavioral inhibition; so convinced that anticipated negative outcomes will happen, people avoid experiences. The inhibition provides a sense of safety, but has two negative consequences. The first is that the people are cut off from what potentially could be meaningful or enjoyable life activities. Second, they miss opportunities for growth and new experiences that might be able to modify negative experiences. This defensive "safe haven" maintains the pathology.

Since Bruce anticipates rejection everywhere and this restricts social contact, there is another common consequence. A person who rarely attends gatherings and never initiates social interaction is likely to be seen as disinterested — a loner, a snob, or a grump. Often others are likely to start treating the person in the very manner anticipated — with rejection.

Bruce's negative schema — his belief in his own worthlessness — is self-fulfilling.

### Does Time Heal All Wounds?

Let's consider a metaphor: Most physical injuries heal, and heal to a degree that years later — or even days later — actual physical pain is completely gone. This physical healing takes place because of complex biological mechanisms that restore normal function. And healing is facilitated by proper care and medical treatment following an injury.

But the effects of physical injury can be long-lasting. Inadequate recovery may be due to impaired immune functioning; improper treatment can lead to complications (deterioration, secondary infections, bones that do not grow back in proper alignment); and repeated reinjuries may retard recovery. In such cases, the initial problem produces long-term consequences. In the realm of emotional injuries, I think it's helpful to see these consequences as falling into two categories: persistence of actual pain and changes in perception and behavior.

If you burn your hand, it starts to heal. Yet if you repeatedly knock the scab off, the wound can stay active indefinitely. Active emotional wounds often remain open, too, as people are reexposed to psychologically destructive relationships and situations. Especially common is the tendency to seek out relationships that replicate maladaptive damaging patterns of interaction experienced early in life.

Some physical injuries are so devastating that even in spite of proper care and some healing, the pain persists. It may only hurt when you bump into something that touches that spot. Or it may be one of those wounds that causes persistent, constant aching. This may be true for some kinds of emotional injuries, as well. Recalling emotionally difficult events touches on and reactivates the old pain. Memories and haunting images of the past have the power to reignite the pain of old wounds. However, *most* people do not experience a lot of direct suffering from specific memories of early life events. The past has left its mark primarily by way of enduring schemas. These persistent beliefs often lie dormant until some current life event reactivates them. For example, a person with underlying *failure* and *incompetency* schemas may not be continuously aware of such issues. However, if they encounter a current-day event that is construed as a failure, the schema comes to life. It then operates to alter cognitive processes and accounts for what can be seen as intense or exaggerated negative feelings, and a multitude of negative, pessimistic congnitions ("I'm so damned stupid! I can't do anything right!").

### ❖ Targets for Treatment

Distorted, negative, and unrealistic cognitions account for a good deal of *unnecessary pain* (as described in Chapter 3). Cognitive behavioral approaches to psychotherapy take aim at this phenomenon. Like a cagey attorney who can spot inconsistencies in a witness's story, cognitive therapists become experts at noticing unrealistic or flawed thinking, and use intervention techniques designed to reduce distortions and to promote more rational thinking. A number of recent cognitive-behavioral therapists have emphasized, however, that in clients with pervasive and rigid maladaptive schemas, the underlying schema must be addressed and modified if one is to be able to have a meaningful impact on distorted cognitions. Approaches that address this issue are discussed in later chapters.

## *Schemas: Active, Dormant, or Extinct*

Many self-schemas lie dormant and may have little impact on one's life, except at times of particular psychological stresses. Obviously, people show vastly different emotional responses to very similar stressful events. An important question to ask each client is, "What is there about this particular event that has been especially painful (or has hit an emotional nerve)?" This search for the *personal meaning* in a stressful event often leads to a greater understanding regarding underlying schemas.

An example serves to illustrate: Robert is a middle-aged accountant. On a day-in, day-out basis he feels relatively confident and competent in his work. He knows his job well and manages to stick to routine tasks in which he is generally successful. However, just recently he made a major error on a project and was criticized rather strongly by his boss. And it's getting to him a lot; he has been ruminating about the reprimand; he has developed tension headaches and restless sleep; and he seems now to be riddled with self-doubts. One might hypothesize that he has an underlying failure/incompetency schema that has been ignited by the event. In most situations, this inner self-schema is avoided and warded off, but now it has come to life.

Let's consider a continuum:

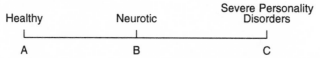

At one end (A) the individual has some underlying schemas that can be judged as benign. The person may previously have experienced conflicts involving these self-schemas, but was able to work through the difficulties and grow beyond them. When confronted with current painful life experiences, he or she is likely to react in an appropriate emotional manner, but not in an exaggerated or uniquely intense way. (If such a person seeks therapy, he or she will likely be diagnosed as experiencing a phase-of-life problem, uncomplicated bereavement, or an adjustment disorder.) These healthy people respond to events in ways that do not activate maladaptive schemas.

At position (B) on the continuum, we see individuals like Robert (above) who only *occasionally* have maladaptive schemas activated in response to very specific kinds of stressors.

Finally are those at position (C). Such people generally have a number of very maladaptive schemas, and are prone to having them activated almost continuously by not only tragic experiences, but also by the events of everyday life. In unique ways, these people appear to be exquisitely sensitive, thin-skinned, and vulnerable. Diagnostically, these folks are typically seen as severely neurotic or personally disordered.

## *Summary*

- Enduring beliefs about the self and others are perhaps the most powerful legacy of early life experiences. Schemas wield a powerful control over life in the present by influencing ongoing perceptions and expectations.

- Enduring, negative schemas play a major role in perpetuating maladaptive patterns of relating with others and also account for the tendency to harbor areas of exquisite emotional vulnerability.

# 10 ❖

---

## *The Search for Personal Meanings: Conscious and Unconscious*

In this chapter we discuss key concepts drawn from psychodynamic theory. What does the term *psychodynamic* mean? A psychodynamic perspective embraces three main ideas. The first is a focus on purposes and intentions. At the heart of this perspective is the goal of trying to understand *why* people behave as they do (Michaels, 1990). Most behavior is not considered to be random. Rather, it is believed to occur for a reason, although often the "reason" may not be readily apparent. This concept has been captured in the term *psychic determinism*. *Psychic determinism* holds that one psychological state or response is caused by an earlier psychological state. As an example, the agoraphobic avoids going into the grocery store because he experiences anticipatory anxiety, fearing a panic attack. The avoidant behavior makes sense.

One way to integrate this with concepts discussed in Chapter 9 is illustrated in this example: A man feels anxious just prior to giving a talk before a group of 30 people. The anxiety can be understood if we know his underlying cognitions and perceptions. In this example, he thinks "Oh, God. I hate doing this. I'm going to make a complete fool of myself." He anticipates humiliation. His particular cognitions are influenced greatly by his underlying schema. As a child he was repeatedly belittled, criticized, and humiliated by his father. The resulting schema is, "I am a failure. If I try to accomplish something, it will not turn out right and I will feel ashamed and humiliated." He may or may not be aware of the underlying schema (since most schemas are largely outside awareness), but he certainly knows that he feels anxious, and on reflection, he could become aware of the particular thoughts and predictions that accompany his anxiety. This is an example of psychic determinism.

The search for "why" always involves an attempt to understand a clients' unique and highly personal *inner meanings*. It is humanistic in focus since it does not rely on prior assumptions, but is sought by way of inquiry about each client's idiosyncratic and highly unique life experiences, values, and inner beliefs.

A second aspect of the psychodynamic perspective is an appreciation of the fact that people are tremendously complex, and within almost everyone are numerous feelings, thoughts, desires, hopes, beliefs, and values that may, at times, be in conflict. Psychodynamically oriented therapists are quite inclined to see inner (intrapsychic) *conflicts* as a common source of emotional distress. Thus, as people speak about their inner experiences, they are encouraged to introspect and to sort through any and all inner thoughts, feelings, and so on. It is deemed important for each person to "know thyself," and this often involves acknowledging inner conflicts.

The third major concept endorsed by psychodynamic theorists is the role of *unconscious mental processing,* which we will examine in detail.

### ❖ *Conscious and Unconscious Mental Processing*

Some examples of psychic determinism are easy to appreciate (when a client can readily tell us why he or she feels or reacts in a certain way); some behaviors are more mysterious. Many of these are manifest as psychiatric symptoms, quirks of behavior, and inhibitions:

- The exquisitely shy man does not really have a clue why he chooses to maintain a life-style of social isolation, especially since he feels very lonely.

- The anxious young woman has no clear conscious reasons for becoming overwhelmingly anxious when someone casually touches her during a conversation.

- The graduate student cannot understand why he feels terribly crushed by receiving what appear to be minor critical remarks on his term paper.

In each case, the person is responding to certain life events, but the subjective experience is complicated by a sense of confusion. These people may be quite perplexed by their reactions, "Why do I feel this way? It doesn't make sense." Or, "Why are my feelings so strong?" And they may feel at the mercy of forces beyond their control, as they encounter strong emotional responses. Many people who seek out psychological treatment are plagued by such experiences. They report experiencing intense or exaggerated emotional reactions that seem disproportionate to the situation. Or they complain of feelings or behaviors that seem odd, irrational, or "crazy." Their lack of understanding of these experiences often results in increased anxiety. Most people are not comfortable with ambiguity, and thus this additional source of worry compounds their sense of subjective distress. In addition, when people are motivated to behave in certain ways or when they experience strong emotions but do not understand why, this can contribute to a general sense of powerlessness and loss of control. Powerlessness/helplessness to some degree accompanies almost all types of psychiatric disorders, and is a major source of emotional suffering.

Let's consider some basic assumptions regarding conscious and unconscious mental phenomena. To be conscious simply means to be "in awareness." It is certainly possible, and very common for people not to be conscious of certain things, and yet behaviorally or emotionally to respond without awareness. A good example occurs when driving for long distances on the highway. Drivers may be absorbed in inner thoughts, and rather oblivious to what they have seen on the road during the past 20 minutes. On a conscious level, they honestly can't recall what they have passed on the highway for the past 20 miles. And yet, some amount of perception and information processing must certainly occur in order to drive safely; but most of it was perceived "unconsciously" (not in full awareness), and the perceptions enabled each driver to stay in his or her lane, pass other cars, and maintain a steady speed. In this example, should a suddenly dangerous situation occur, this would immediately be registered at a conscious level; infused with affect, the perception would motivate evasive action.

Thus, one assumption is that people are capable of perceiving and cognitively processing events on at least two levels (in awareness and outside awareness) and both levels of processing can provoke responses. The responses can occur on four levels: (1) emotional reactions; (2) behavioral responses (e.g., withdrawal, escape, avoidance); (3) somatic sensations; and (4) effects on cognitive functioning (e.g., increase alertness and vigilance; influence the interpretation of events in accord with underlying schemas; provoke selective inattention). Figure 10-A illustrates how a stimulus event is registered at both conscious and unconscious levels, and how each level of processing can provoke a response.

Certain aspects of a stimulus event are more readily processed consciously (this commonly includes the words others speak or what one hopes and wants to perceive) while other aspects of the experience are processed

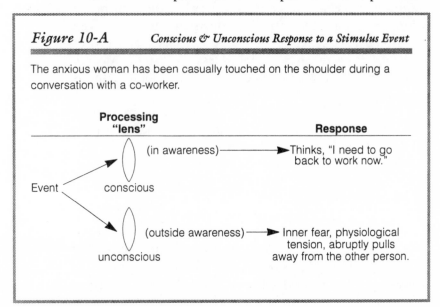

*Figure 10-A*     *Conscious & Unconscious Response to a Stimulus Event*

The anxious woman has been casually touched on the shoulder during a conversation with a co-worker.

unconsciously (often such data are more affective in nature, such as information conveyed via facial expressions, vocal tone, and body language). Often, but not always, conscious experiences are analyzed via conceptual processing, while preconscious or unconscious material is encoded by way of experiential processing (see Chapter 8).

The unconscious perception/processing, occurs without awareness; the resulting *response*, however, may or may not be noticed consciously. It may go completely unnoticed; it may register as a vaguely felt sense of uneasiness; or she may clearly feel a surge of tension and anxiety, but not really know why.

Let's consider another example — Figure 10-B — that highlights this same process and illustrates one form of intrapsychic conflict that can occur when different elements of an event are processed at different levels. In this example, a woman who has been experiencing her husband as being more distant asks him, "Do you still love me?" The figure illustrates her perception of his response at the conscious and unconscious levels.

*Figure 10-B*          *Conscious & Unconscious Processing of a Stimulus Event*

| Event | Elements of the Event | Processing "Lens" | Derived Meaning | Inner Response | In Awareness |
|---|---|---|---|---|---|
| Comment From Husband | "You know that I love you." | conscious | He loves me (conceptual) | I should be reassured that he loves me. | Yes |
| | Vocal tone and facial expression suggest insincerity. | unconscious | He seems cold, distant, and insincere. He is not being honest (experiential) | Disappointed, sad, angry | * |

\* If this aspect of her response is outside her awareness, two consequences are likely. First, rather than feel the underlying emotions directly, she will probably experience only a vague felt sense of tension, distress, or uneasiness (an inner unpleasant feeling that is hard for her to define). Many people enter psychotherapy with similar complaints of ill-defined dysphoria for which they can offer little explanation. A second likely consequence is that the underlying perception will motivate behavior such as clinginess, or, conversely, an urge to back off and maintain distance. However, her behavioral response may not feel willful or volitional, and again, she may not fully understand her own reactions.

###  *Why Are Some Aspects of Mental Life Unconscious?*

The most simple reason that experiences are processed at an unconscious level is that they are unimportant and not deserving of our attention (irrelevant background sensations; the boring scene along the highway during the long drive). Such inattention is essential since it would be impossible consciously to attend to the multitude of stimuli bombarding us each minute of the day.

When stimulus events are compelling they are much more likely to be noticed. Thus, events that pose potential dangers to survival are immediately registered and grab attention. Likewise, personally meaningful stimuli will be noticed by some while ignored by others (this is influenced by one's particular interests and concerns, such as a pregnant woman who readily notices advertisements for baby food, and events that touch on core schemas).

Another very common reason that processing occurs on an unconscious level is that inner experiences have not been subject to conceptual processing or verbalization. This issue requires some discussion. Let's begin with a common illustration.

A man comes home from work and seems out of sorts. His wife notices this and asks him, "Is there anything wrong?"

> Man: *No, not really.*
> Wife: *Well you seem kind of tense; are you sure nothing is bothering you?*
> Man: *I don't think so.*

Like a good therapist, his wife decides not to accept his initial response as the final word; she probes:

> Wife: *Well, what happened today?*
> Man: *Well, Jerry came in and dumped this load of work on my desk right when I was about to leave, and said it needed to be completed this week. He's done this before and it really irritates me.*
> Wife: *Maybe that's what I was sensing in you.*
> Man: *Yeah, I guess it is bugging me.*

With the slightest encouragement to speak aloud about the events of the day, the man is able to put his finger on something that had, in fact, upset him.

His emotions were largely out of awareness, although he may have sensed some discomfort. Thinking about and reviewing the events of the day and prompted to talk about it, facilitated a process that helped him become clearer about how he felt. Language is a mediator of experience that can help translate vaguely felt inner experiences into a more easily acknowledged and clearer sense of what one has perceived or what one feels. Such underlying, unconscious cognitions and feelings are certainly not deeply "repressed." They are on the edge of awareness, and can be illuminated via the processes of reflecting, thinking, and — especially — verbal articulation. Dim inner sensations may remain as estranged, unarticulated, undifferentiated experiences until verbalizing brings clarity and coherence to the inner experience (Shapiro, 1989).

Some inner experiences remain largely unconscious (or preconscious) because the underlying sensations, images, or emotions are so foreign to the person that it is difficult to find any way to represent these experiences in language. This is especially so when the inner experiences being evoked involve primitive affective states or when they are being felt by people who typically are very unaccustomed to feeling emotions (e.g., rigid, obsessional individuals).

Finally, some inner mental experiences remain out of awareness intentionally, because of defensive operations. Such unconscious material is *actively avoided* because if it were noticed consciously, it would create some form of distress.

Let's consider an example: A man has grown up heavily invested in maintaining an image of rugged self-reliance. Early life experiences included shaming if he were to show any sign of emotional weakness. Thus a core schema developed: "If I am needy or emotional, I will be criticized and rejected by others, and will feel humiliated." In midlife, his wife is killed in an automobile accident. Inwardly, he is beset by waves of sadness and loneliness. Since such emotions are not acceptable to him, they are defended against. His inner pain is barred from consciousness. In a very real sense, he is not aware of his internal despair. What he mainly notices is a pain in his chest (heartache?), constant tension, and an increased urge to drink alcohol.

In such cases, a host of defense mechanisms may be employed to maintain the lack of awareness. Presumably the anticipated pain of feelings of humiliation motivate this self-protective stance. Yet he pays a price. Cut off from his human feelings of loss (necessary pain) he is not able to truly mourn his loss.

 ### *Prices Paid*

When important inner experiences remain at an unconscious level, several undesirable consequences may occur:

- Undifferentiated and vague emotional states and somatic symptoms result in discomfort and often perplexity. The lack of awareness and understanding of these reactions, as noted earlier, can leave people feeling confused and powerless.

- Unconscious perceptions may motivate behavioral inhibition (e.g., the person who has not worked through a traumatic loss may shy away from any personal involvement or attachments, and this may be done in a very automatic way — without conscious choice or volition). This is a major reason many people feel "stuck" in their lives, unable to pursue important life activities, unable to spread their wings and grow.

- Unaware of inner "truths," people are less able to make informed choices or to take decisive actions. People may agree to do things that they do not really want to do, or fail to act in assertive ways in relationships.

- Excessive repression interferes with the processes of working through that are essential components of emotional healing.

- Extreme defensiveness can, and often does, lead to a state of devitalization, emptiness, and an impoverished sense of self.

## ❖ *Treatment Implications*

For many of our clients, a major stumbling block that interferes with emotional healing and growth can be traced to the problems we have just discussed. Thus, a major focus in some psychotherapies will be to facilitate increased accurate awareness of both external events and internal experiences. This goal is at the heart of psychodynamic approaches and has often been referred to as a process of fostering *insight*. Achieving greater insight is much more than an intellectual procedure. What it really involves are:

- Getting clear about what really matters

- Gathering as much accurate information as possible regarding external realities and inner truths (needs, beliefs, feelings) so one may make wise choices and act in accord with one's true self.

- Accessing underlying needs and emotions, in order to experience these more fully, which can facilitate emotional healing.

## ❖ *Understanding The Past*

Psychodynamic approaches to treatment have often been accused of focusing too much on clients' childhood experiences. At times exploration of early life events can become a stilted exercise that is overintellectualized and in the service of resistance. Also, the knowledge of painful childhood experiences can be used as an excuse for not growing or coping, or ammunition to induce guilt in others. However, in my experience, two very important things can often occur as our clients come to know more fully the experiences of their early lives.

Let us return to the earlier example of the man who lost his wife in an automobile accident: As he begins in therapy to notice intensely painful feelings of sadness, he also encounters feelings of shame and humiliation. However, he and his therapist have also spoken about his early life. It has become increasingly clear to him that his father was profoundly harsh and inappropriate in dishing out criticism and shaming remarks. Having a more complete understanding of these early experiences has helped him in two ways. First, he now has a more realistic perspective which helps him understand why he has been so afraid to express his feelings. In the context of his early family, to do so was not safe and carried considerable emotional risk. He now can appreciate this part of himself more fully. Second, and most important, knowledge of his early experiences has helped him to adopt a more compassionate attitude toward himself. In one session he commented, "It is understandable to me that I feel so uneasy about crying. If I'd done so when I was a kid, I would have been raked over the coals. But, I have lost my wife, I'm terribly sad, I loved her dearly," and he begins to cry (he can now own his pain, acknowledge his humanness, and he can weep without shame).

Psychiatrist Robert Michaels (1990) has said that one common outcome of psychotherapy is that clients rewrite their histories (as they come to know more clearly a more complete and balanced picture of how they experienced the past). Figure 10-C includes several examples that illustrate this point.

### Figure 10-C

| Older Version | Newer Version |
| --- | --- |
| I was a hopeless victim. | I experienced considerable emotional pain and I was courageous. I was able to endure, and against the odds, I survived. |
| I was a pitiful, whining, cry baby. | I was a little kid with absolutely legitimate needs and I had the misfortune to be born into a family with parents who were incapable of nurturing. |
| My God-damned mother ruined my life. | My mother did things to me that no child deserved, and I know now that a lot of this was due to her own mental illness. |
| I was worthless; I couldn't even protect my younger brother and sister from a tyrannical, alcoholic father, and a completely unavailable mother. | Of course it was impossible for a 10-year-old child to take over the role of parent to two younger sibs. I did my best, but it was an unrealistic and impossible expectation for a young child. |

In my view none of the concepts in this chapter, drawn from psychodynamic approaches to discovering meaning, are incompatible with either cognitive or humanistic models of psychotherapy. Each of these models focuses on particular aspects of human psychology; each has something to offer as we undertake the complex task of helping clients to heal and to grow.

### ❖ *Summary*

- Central to psychodynamic approaches is the interest in helping clients to *get clear* about and to *own* inner "truths." At the heart of this is encouragement to discover uniquely felt personal meanings surrounding particular events and internal experiences.

- Understanding something about the past and how it has influenced the development of a person has a far greater impact than merely achieving "insight." One of the most important consequences from more fully understanding one's past is to be able to appreciate inner feelings, needs, and sensitivities from a perspective of greater self-compassion.

# Contributions From Humanistic Psychology

*Advances in knowledge will... bring about the gradual demise of "schools" of psychotherapy.*

— Carl Rogers (1961)

The humanistic approach to psychotherapy has put the *therapeutic relationship* center stage; it is seen as *the* primary vehicle promoting psychological growth and healing. The success of such a relationship is grounded in essential human qualities such as empathy, congruence, and genuine positive regard (Kelly, 1997).

The establishment of a warm, supportive, and empathic environment between client and therapist has been widely embraced, by various schools of therapy, as an essential ingredient in psychological healing. For instance, Stiles et al. (1996) found that this variable was ranked highly (second in a list of 19 treatment techniques or interactions) by both psychodynamic and cognitive-behavioral therapists. Suffice it to say that a decent, respectful, and caring human interaction is the essential foundation for any successful psychotherapy.

Rogers believed that early experiences with important others have a profound effect on the growth of the self. In an atmosphere of positive regard and acceptance, a child can begin movement toward the development of his or her unique, authentic self. Conversely, harshness, lack of love, and nonacceptance can derail this process. This general notion is certainly in keeping with both psychodynamic and cognitive (schema) theories. Rogers also adopted an optimistic perspective regarding human potential. He believed in an innate striving toward health and growth. A part of the process of psychotherapy is to encourage openness to inner subjective experiences as a means of reconnecting the client to his or her inner and often unactualized self. This is aided by providing deep caring, respect, and empathetic experiences that Rogers believed were powerful forces promoting growth (Rogers, 1961).

### ❖ *Stages of Psychological Growth*

Rogers provided an exceptionally clear description of psychological change that is commonly encountered as people go through psychotherapy. Central to this process is movement from a state of *remoteness from experience to one of awareness and acceptance of experience* (Rogers, 1961). He describes seven stages (Greenberg et al. 1993, pp. 37-38).

**Stage 1.**   The client is largely unaware of inner subjective feelings, needs, and so on, and is unwilling to share personal experiences. Often at this stage, the client maintains distance in the relationship with the therapist, seeing openness as threatening. Beliefs about the self are quite rigid.

**Stage 2.**   The beginning expression of emotions and personal cognitions, but often such expressions are not owned. Inner subjective experiences are felt as contradictory, confusing, and alien.

**Stage 3.**   Increasing expression of inner emotions and thoughts, but these are either shared in a stilted way (talked about in the past tense, or in an over-intellectualized manner) or seen by the client as very unacceptable. Personal beliefs (self-schemas) continue to be inflexible, but clients may begin to question their validity. There may be more awareness of contradictions in inner values, beliefs, and feelings.

**Stage 4.**   Increased   ability   and   willingness   to acknowledge emotions experienced in the moment and greater sense of ownership of inner experiences. There is a gradual shift toward more acceptance of inner subjective feelings, hunches, and ideas. Introjected "scripts" or "shoulds" that are not congruent with one's own feelings or values are beginning to be questioned.

**Stage 5.** Feelings and personal thoughts are now more openly and freely expressed. A transformation is occurring as the client takes such inner experiences more seriously, seeing them in valid and valued aspects of the self. There is movement toward an increased desire to be true to one's self.

**Stage 6.** Feelings are now expressed with more immediacy. There is less hesitancy, more spontaneity, and more acceptance of inner experiences simply being "the truth." Inner "data" are now considered to be very important as people engage in problem-solving and make important life decisions. Often clients will report that they are *feeling* more emotional pain (as they are increasingly aware of the truth of inner emotions), but the feelings are seen as understandable and are easier to face and accept. Often clients report feeling more "real" and more "alive." Introjected "scripts" are now being rewritten in accord with one's own life experiences and personal values. The self feels more authentic.

**Stage 7.** At this level, the client has come to trust in his or her own inner experiences as an important guide for living. There is marked decrease in internal conflict and increased openness to new experiences.

These stages represent not only emotional growth in a general sense, but also a progressive development of the self. The two critical ingredients are: *fostering increasing openness and awareness of inner subjective experience* (a concept not unlike that encouraged by psychoanalysis) and *providing a tremendously accepting and supportive interpersonal relationship* for such openness to occur. Growth can only occur in an atmosphere of safety. This concept is at the heart of humanistic approaches, but certainly not exclusive to that model.

### ❖ *Healing Relationships*

In the 1940s psychoanalyst Franz Alexander coined the term *corrective emotional experience*. This referred to *the* critical ingredient in a therapeutic relationship that fostered healing, growth, and change. This concept has often been seen in an oversimplistic way to mean the provision of a generally positive, supportive interaction. But Alexander was describing something more than just a benign interaction (1946).

People growing up in conditions of significant emotional abuse, neglect, and so on, clearly are harmed by such experiences (especially if pervasive and long lasting). "Common sense" suggests that someone raised by an abusive parent would gravitate toward healthier people as soon as he or she is able to leave home. But, of course, this frequently does not happen. Rather — counterintuitively — one legacy of early harmful interactions with others, is the tendency to seek out similar interactions with others after leaving the family of origin (a phenomenon sometimes referred to as the *repetition compulsion*). When this occurs, emotional hurts continue and core schemas go unaltered, or are even reinforced.

For a therapeutic relationship to be a truly "corrective experience," it must be generally supportive and accepting, but it must also *not repeat the destructive pattern of early hurtful relationships*. And that, as many experienced therapists will attest, is not always easy to do.

All good therapists have the intention to help and not hurt their clients. Yet many clients commonly, inadvertently act in ways that evoke toxic reactions from others (including from therapists). Two clinical examples will illustrate this point:

- The extremely passive, dependent person was raised in a family where the frequent message was "you can't do anything. You are inadequate. You can't stand on your own two feet. You don't have what it takes." This person enters therapy and comes across in the first session as so profoundly wounded and helpless, that it elicits certain responses from the therapist.

(Let's be honest, this has happened to all of us! With good intentions, we take the bait and respond by giving advice, not stopping the session on time, or in other ways treating the client like a helpless infant. This, unfortunately, repeats the experience of being treated as an inadequate person. If this continues, the client may feel "taken care of," but won't grow.)

- The intensely volatile, hostile, bitter, degrading borderline client assaults the therapist with disparaging comments. The therapist, her button pushed, becomes curt and defensive. The client storms out of the session, once again convinced, "Even this therapist dislikes me. People are just no damned good!"

- For a therapeutic relationship to be helpful, it must be supportive and empathic. It also requires that the therapist monitor his or her own countertransference and avoid taking the bait (being sucked into repeating hurtful patterns of interaction with the client).

### Keeping the Faith

First and foremost in Rogers's model is the belief in an inherent *growth tendency* — the healing potential within each person. Even in terribly wounded individuals there remains an underlying desire and potential to heal and to grow. Especially with profoundly psychologically damaged clients, the therapist's consistent (but also realistic) hopefulness may be one of the most important elements of psychotherapy, helping to sustain clients through periods of suffering, discouragement, and hopelessness.

*Summary*

- The foundation for healing relationships lies in the quality of the interpersonal relationship. But a healing relationship is not simply defined as being a nice or benign person. Critical to developing such a relationship is an appreciation for the unique life experiences of each individual client, and being able to offer a "corrective experience."

- Carl Rogers has given us a good generic map to track stages of change often witnessed in the course of psychotherapy.

# 12 ❖

# The Mind and the Brain: A Neurobiological Perspective

*The mind is what the brain does.*
— Francis Crick, Nobel laureate

The 1990s have been designated as the *decade of the brain,* and rightly so, as we have witnessed an explosion of new discoveries in the neurosciences. Many of these have been ushered in by the advent of new technologies that have expanded the capacity to explore functioning in living brains. In addition, pharmacological research, as well as clinical experience, have resulted in more sophisticated theories of brain functioning and safer medical treatments for a host of psychiatric illnesses.

Although currently the medical treatment of mental and emotional disorders is limited to physicians (and in some states, nurse practitioners), it is important for all mental health professionals to know about the signs and symptoms that alert the clinician to the presence of a medication-responsive psychiatric illness. In this chapter we take a brief look at several important issues regarding brain functioning and psychological disorders. In Chapter 13 we address diagnostic issues relevant to medication treatment. And in Chapter 19 we see how psychopharmacology can be an important aspect of effective brief treatment with some clients.

### ❖ The Emotional Brain

In the core of the brain lies the *limbic system* and a related brain structure, the *hypothalamus* (see Figure 12-A). Together these brain structures make up what is commonly referred to as the emotional brain. This is an appropriate designation, for these brain structures, in complex ways, influence emotions and emotional behaviors in two broad ways. First, the limbic system (which includes the septum, the cingulate gyrus, the hippocampus, and the amygdala) can be seen as the launching site for felt emotions. When people (and lower level organisms, for that matter) "feel" an emotion, this sensation is elicited by chemical events emanating from one or more of the limbic structures. A microsecond later this is followed by the release of a host of stress hormones (by way of the hypothalamus, the pituitary gland, and the autonomic nervous system).

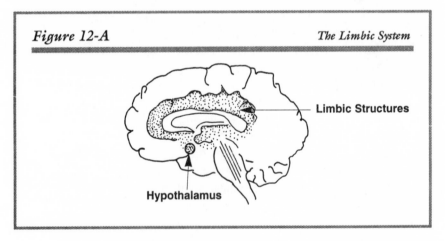

*Figure 12-A*                              *The Limbic System*

— Limbic Structures

Hypothalamus

In addition, the limbic system plays a crucial role in the mediation and control of emotions. On a neurobiological level, these brain structures operate to contain or to modulate emotional expression. Many forms of major psychiatric illness involve emotional dyscontrol; often, at least a part of this may be traced to malfunctions in limbic circuits.

Proper functioning of these primitive brain structures relies on a very complex interaction of many neurochemicals (neurotransmitters, neuromodulators, and hormones). Current theories regarding the biology of mental illnesses have focused largely on neurochemical dysfunctions in the brain and abnormalities of nerve cell functioning. As we begin to take a look at malfunctions in the emotional brain, let us consider four main pathways to disordered brain functioning, which may play an important role in the lives of our clients.

## Pathways to Brain Dysfunction

Pathway number one is by way of *genetic transmission.* Several major mental illnesses have been found to run in families, and have a presumed, underlying genetic basis. Having flawed genetics, at least in the realm of psychiatric disorders, does not mean that all offspring will manifest a particular disorder. But it does mean that such children are at higher risk for developing certain syndromes. At times, genetic predispositions may require certain environmental triggers to initiate the disease process. One example of this is the theory of *kindling* in which psychosocial stressors or sympathomimetic drug abuse may ignite the first one or two episodes of bipolar disorder, which thereafter becomes more of an autonomous biological disorder. Disorders currently felt to be influenced by genetic factors include bipolar illness, schizophrenia, attention deficit disorder, to some extent alcoholism, some forms of unipolar depression, and obsessive compulsive disorder. Often these more biologically based disorders are clearly complicated by environmental, interpersonal, cognitive, and other "psychological" issues (and thus there is a role for psychotherapy), although the primary "cause" may be traced to abnormalities of brain chemistry. For this reason, psychotropic medication is generally the treatment of choice.

*Temperamental or constitutional factors* can also significantly affect brain functioning. These may be manifest in persistent difficulties with affect regulation, impulsivity, rejection or separation sensitivity, excessive risk avoidance, heightened autonomic arousal, or pathological stimulus-seeking behavior. These temperamental "styles" may or may not be inherited, and can be seen in the context of otherwise emotionally healthy, nurturing family environments.

A third type of neurobased problem is considered to be *acquired brain dysfunction*. Let's consider two versions of this type of dysfunction. The first are acquired brain injuries associated with neurological trauma, the effects of toxins (including substance abuse), and disease. Diseases can include both primary brain diseases (for example, Alzheimer's disease or encephalitis) and systemic diseases that secondarily affect brain functioning (such as hypothyroidism or renal failure). A second group of acquired brain disorders have received a good deal of attention lately: more or less permanent brain disorders that can be traced to the effects of severe or prolonged stress.

Acquired brain dysfunctions have been documented in survivors of severe child abuse and in adults that have experienced prolonged states of fear and powerlessness (for example, war veterans suffering with post-traumatic stress disorder (PTSD)). The brain changes noted are seen both on a microscopic/cellular and chemical level and in changes in actual brain morphology. Some of these changes include chronic alterations in certain neurotransmitter systems (e.g., norepinephrine and serotonin) and stress hormones (e.g., chronically elevated levels of glucocorticoids), and atrophy of the hippocampal gyri. Such brain changes may account for a portion of the difficulty that clinicians encounter when treating disorders such as borderline personality disorder, chronic PTSD, and some forms of persistent depression. Details regarding research in this area are beyond the scope of this book, but the reader is referred to van der Kolk et al. (1996), Silk (1994), and Preston (1997) for a more comprehensive discussion.

Finally, in addition to more or less permanent changes in brain functioning, as just described, many of our clients suffer from relatively transient changes in neurochemical functioning as a *response to psychosocial stressors*. One very common example of this is seen in reactive depressions. In many individuals, in addition to psychological symptoms of depression, we also see the emergence of certain physical symptoms that can serve as markers of an underlying neurochemical dysregulation (e.g., sleep disorders, decreased libido, appetite changes, and excessive fatigue, to mention a few). These symptoms may subside as psychological stresses are resolved, or they may persist for months, as the initial "reactive" disorder has taken on more of an autonomous biological life of its own. These *stress-induced neurochemical disorders* certainly can occur in individuals that are genetically at risk, but they can and do also present in otherwise emotionally healthy people, when the stressors are especially severe and prolonged. Another factor, that is discussed in later chapters, is the experience of powerlessness or helplessness and how this can, in a potent way, induce neurobiological and hormonal changes in most people.

## *Treatment Implications*

With each and every client we must always be watchful for particular signs that alert the clinician to the possibility of an underlying neurochemical problem. This is generally gleaned when taking a careful history of the individual, as well as a history of emotional problems in blood relatives, and an assessment for the presence or absence of key symptoms (this is explored in detail in Chapter 13).

## *Summary*

- Regardless of one's theoretical orientation, all psychotherapists must be alert to the possibility that certain clients present with disorders that can be traced in part or in full to neurochemical dysfunction in the nervous system. Failure to attend to this issue can result not only in prolonged and unnecessary suffering for some clients, but may also leave the clinician vulnerable to malpractice suits.

- Human psychological functioning is so complex that unitary explanatory models are simply inadequate. There is always an interactive, two-way street between the brain and the mind.

# PART THREE

---

# *Assessment: Understanding the Client*

To begin Part Three let's consider a metaphor, comparing psychotherapy with a journey taken by the early pioneers. Before embarking on what may be a difficult journey it's probably a good idea to consider the following:

- Know where you want to go and why you want to make the trip.

- Determine if this particular trip is realistic given your time, energy, resources, and the degree of risk.

- Take stock of your strengths and weaknesses.

- Know something about travel in general (especially how to navigate through unfamiliar territory.)

- Be prepared for road blocks, detours, and danger along the way (and know how to respond).

- Figure out an appropriate pace.

- Know what to do (in general) if you get lost.

- Know when you have arrived (or that you have gone far enough).

- Finally, the journey is more likely to be successful if you are accompanied by a guide who is familiar with the territory.

Assessment is the first step in the journey. In this section we consider a number of issues that relate to understanding our clients and that are important in making critical decisions regarding treatment. We look at three broad areas: *diagnostic issues,* the *nature of presenting problems,* and the *assessment of specific psychological liabilities* (which will become the target for specific treatment interventions).

**113**

# Diagnostic Maps

The assessment of a client's strengths and weaknesses is an ongoing process, obviously subject to periodic shifts as our understanding of their dynamics and their unique characterological issues become clearer. However, when conducting brief therapy, it is quite important to arrive at some initial diagnostic impressions during the first one or two sessions. This is critical if we are to accomplish anything during shorter-term treatments.

Diagnostic assessment is much more than an academic activity or a dehumanizing exercise aimed at securing an appropriate label. Accurate assessment, I will argue, is essential for at least three important reasons. First, it can give us a map to follow so that the clinician has an idea about the nature of the client's problems and, with this in mind, can decide on appropriate strategies for facilitating change. Second, a clear diagnostic picture helps the therapist to establish reasonable treatment goals (e.g., suitability for brief therapy) and to develop a realistic prognosis. Finally, and very important, the therapist's accurate assessment of the clients' unique dynamics can contribute to her experience of feeling understood by the therapist, which is so crucial for developing a working alliance in the treatment relationship.

In this chapter we outline and discuss five important diagnostic issues (or perspectives) to consider in each and every case.

## ❖ *Overview of "Diagnostic Maps"*

- Client's level of functioning

- Level of interpersonal relatedness

- Personality styles

- Signs and symptoms of possible neurobiological dysfunction

- Client characteristics relevant to the prognosis, treatment planning, and suitability for brief therapy

## ❖ *The Fundamental Assessment Issue: The Client's Level of Functioning*

All therapists must be aware that psychotherapy can be a powerful experience. Treatment can be beneficial, but as therapy outcome studies attest, it can also be harmful. Many factors must be considered as one chooses both general and specific treatment strategies, but first and foremost is the assessment of a client's level of ego functioning. I believe this to be the fundamental assessment issue.

### *To "Open Up" or to Stabilize? That Is the Question*

All successful therapies are built on the bedrock of a solid, trusting, safe, and compassionate relationship. Beyond this essential helping relationship, intervention strategies and theoretical models vary considerably. One classical way to describe the basic approaches to psychotherapy is to see them taking one of two major paths: (1) Insight-oriented therapy, or (2) treatment that aims more for emotional stabilization, and more successful coping with daily life (a type of treatment traditionally called "supportive therapy").

Before addressing assessment per se, let's elaborate a bit on these two important approaches to treatment.

Pathway number one generally has been referred to as expressive, exploratory, uncovering, or insight-oriented psychotherapy. Its goal is to help the client to increase his or her awareness of inner experiences (e.g., awareness of needs, longings, feelings, and uniquely felt personal meanings, values, and beliefs). This may also include approaches designed to increase understanding (e.g., coming to know more about one's behaviors, making sense of past experiences, getting clear about inner truths). Techniques and interventions in this vein operate to heighten and intensify experience. They elicit responses, invite reflection, and encourage openness.

Such techniques are not inherently good or bad; it all depends. If these interventions take place prematurely with a constricted, inhibited, neurotic client, the fear of intense emotions or the experience of shame and vulnerability may lead to a hasty departure from treatment. However, timed well and balanced with sensitivity and care, these approaches may be the critical ingredient in treating overdefended, very rigid neurotic clients. Conversely, expressive approaches are frequently risky with people who have marginal ego functioning (e.g., severely traumatized individuals or those with personality disorders). It may surely "open them up," but to volcanic emotions and internal chaos.

Pathway number two is the road to containment. Strategies here aim to decrease arousal, foster affective stabilization, and improve adaptive self-control. In a sense, the treatment is aimed at shoring up and strengthening a fragile ego. This approach has often been called *supportive psychotherapy*, although this term may not be the best to describe such treatment. All psychotherapy is (or should be) supportive. And too often, the concept of supportive therapy brings to mind images of hand-holding or baby-sitting. (Ultimately, successful treatments for all clients aim to avoid infantilization, and strive to empower and foster growth and autonomy.) I prefer to call these approaches *stabilizing interventions*. All techniques subsumed under this general heading are designed to improve ego functioning (to enhance emotional control, improve thinking and problem-solving, and increase reality testing), and to foster the development of more adaptive coping strategies. In part, this also requires an active avoidance of interventions that promote regression or heighten arousal (Preston, 1997).

There are many clients who are undeniably high-functioning, mentally healthy folks. Other clients have obvious, severe ego impairment. However, with a fair number of the people we see the picture is not this clear. Some clients, for example, look more fragile than they really are. Others superficially have personas that bespeak of higher level functioning, but which are only thin veneers, hiding underlying borderline pathology. In some cases, these clients with less apparent strengths or those with hidden psychopathology may be harder to spot during the first few therapy sessions. Thus, the clinician must be alert to subtle indicators, and become adept at ferreting out both hidden strengths and underlying liabilities.

## Ego Functioning

One of the most useful of the models that address the issue of level functioning and emotional vulnerability is the *ego function model*. This model is an outgrowth of psychoanalytic theory, but, in my view, it is a perspective that is acceptable to many therapists, even those disinclined to think in psychodynamic terms. The model was developed and refined by Bellack and colleagues (1973).

## Resistance to Dysfunction

Let's begin this section with a brief discussion of the concept of *ego strength*. In general terms, ego strength refers to the degree of emotional durability and adaptability a person exhibits (especially in the face of significant psychosocial stressors). It is best seen in terms of *resistance to dysfunction* and *resiliency*. Resistance to dysfunction implies that even when confronted with serious stressors, the person with well-developed ego strength continues to function and does not emotionally collapse. This is not to suggest that such people do not experience emotional suffering — quite the contrary. People with strong egos absolutely do experience and express a full range of human emotions during crises. In fact, their ability to experience and express feelings appropriately (e.g., sadness, anger, joy, and so on) is one sign of their personality strength. However, such emotions are expressed in a mature and well-modulated fashion. So, at times of even intensely painful life events, high-functioning people may suffer a great deal, but they are still able to cope with major life issues (e.g., work, education, parenting, and relationships). As the old Timex commercial put it, these folks can "take a lickin' and keep on tickin'."

## *Resiliency*

*Resiliency* is related to the ability to resist decompensation and dysfunction. All people have limits to what they can endure and in the face of extremely severe or prolonged stressors, some impairment in functioning may occur. Even the strongest among us may become overwhelmed, at least for a while. However, another marker of ego strength is the ability to regroup and recover emotionally when major stressful events subside. This contrasts with those who function at lower levels of ego strength, who may become seriously impaired (often in response even to mild-to-moderate stressors), and who remain quite symptomatic for a prolonged period of time after major stressors subside (this is commonly seen in individuals with serious personality disorders).

Finally, in emotionally resilient people, the clinician will be impressed by the continuing presence of many personal strengths despite tremendous emotional suffering. One should never look solely at the amount of psychic pain as a barometer of ego functioning. We all have the capability of suffering a great deal when life is hard, or tragic, but those with solid egos "keep on tickin'."

*Only with caution lift the lid on the id of the kid*
— Harry Wilmer
*Practical Jung*

### ❖ Assessing Ego Functions

The following parallels the ego function model proposed by Bellack and colleagues (1973). His group speaks of ego functions as existing on a continuum from mature, healthy, and adaptive (level 7) to immature, maladaptive, and grossly pathological (level 1). Let's take a look at this model by first considering the general continuum (see Figure 13-A), and then focusing specifically on four separate ego functions: (1) thought processes, (2) reality testing, (3) defenses, and (4) control of emotions and impulses (particular aspects of these ego functions are summarized in Figure 13-B).

---

**Figure 13-A**                    *Continuum of Personality Functioning*

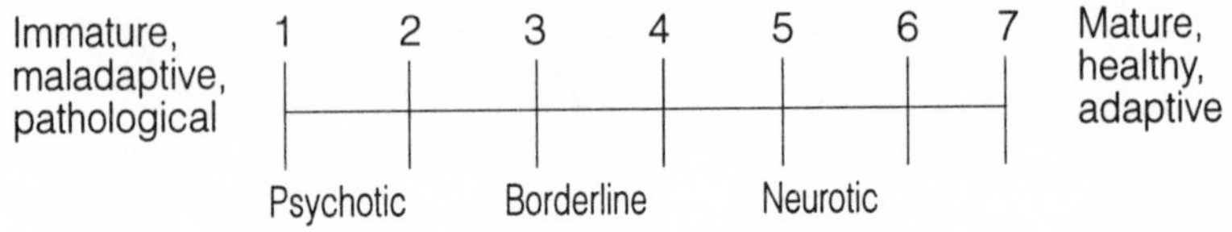

Immature, maladaptive, pathological    1    2    3    4    5    6    7    Mature, healthy, adaptive

Psychotic        Borderline        Neurotic

---

## Figure 13-B

*Ego Functions*

| Level | Thought Processes |
|---|---|
| 6-7 | Logical, realistic thinking. Good ability to problem solve, anticipate consequences. |
| 4-6 | May exhibit concreteness or overgeneralized thinking (especially when under stress), e.g., all-or-none conclusions, arbitrary inferences, pessimistic predictions. However, thinking is logical and goal directed. Errors in thinking at this level include the often cited "cognitive distortions" proposed by Aaron Beck (1976) and other cognitive therapists. |
| 2-4 | More extreme, arbitrary conclusions, lack of critical thinking; thinking tends to be impulsive without appropriate reflectiveness. Can present with magical thinking, ideas of reference, and quasidelusional thinking. |
| 1-2 | Severe fragmentation of thought processes, loose associations, confusion, profoundly unrealistic conclusions, delusions. |

| Level | Reality Testing (and Sense of Reality) |
|---|---|
| 6-7 | Intact reality testing. |
| 4-6 | Intact reality testing in most circumstances, however, some impairments seen in the context of intense relationships (e.g., transference reactions) or strong emotions (e.g., loss of perspective while in the midst of significant emotional arousal). |
| 2-4 | Significant impairments in reality testing, e.g., grossly misreading social cues or interpersonal interactions, jumping to farfetched conclusions. May experience transient illusions or hallucinations. Blurring of self-other boundaries. Derealization. |
| 1-2 | Marked impairment in reality testing. Confusion, hallucinations. |

| Level | Defenses |
|---|---|
| 6-7 | Defenses are employed only during times of intense stress. Defenses used are effective in warding off emotional dyscontrol and involve little or no distortion of reality. Defensive operations typically include mild levels of denial, rationalization, intellectualization, humor, and distractions (e.g., playing sports, exercising, taking a weekend vacation). And, importantly, the degree of defensiveness is not extreme, so the individual can easily access, acknowledge, and express inner feelings when he/she chooses to do so. |

*continued next page...*

*Figure 13-B continued...*                      *Ego Functions*

| | |
|---|---|
| 4-6 | The hallmark of neurosis is an overreliance on defenses, i.e., various intrapsychic and interpersonal maneuvers designed to avoid experiencing or expressing inner emotional pain. |
| 2-4 | Defenses are brittle and often ineffective in warding off intense affective arousal. Defenses often involve significant impairment in reality testing (e.g., denial, projection, splitting, severe distortions). The dominant defenses are collectively referred to as "acting out" (i.e., desperate attempts to avoid awareness of inner emotional pain, such as severe substance abuse, self-mutilation, rampant promiscuity, binge eating, etc.). |
| 1-2 | Marginal or no adequate defenses. |

| Level | Control of Emotions and Impulses |
|---|---|
| 6-7 | Exhibits both the ability to contain and control emotions *appropriately and* to choose to express feelings at the appropriate time and place (i.e., has the capacity to engage in healthy emotional expression, e.g., mourn losses, express frustration, etc.). |
| 4-6 | Two versions are seen at this level. The first is a degree of impaired emotional dyscontrol where the individual feels overwhelmed and may either express emotions in a maladaptive manner or experience a loss of control (e.g., break down crying at work). The second version is maladaptive overcontrol where the individual keeps a lid on emotional expression to an excessive degree. The result is difficulty in sharing feelings with others and a diminished capacity for appropriately working through painful emotional experiences. |
| 2-4 | Again, two versions are seen: The first is severe emotional dysregulation. Individuals are exquisitely sensitive to stressors and respond to them with intense, poorly modulated outbursts of emotion (e.g., intense despair, rage, severe panic). The second version involves desperate attempts to contain intense affects, but it is a sort of brittle control. The overcontrol often gives way to extreme emotional outbursts. In addition, the severe dyscontrol seen at this level may include suicidal, homicidal, and/or self-mutilation behaviors. |
| 1-2 | Marked emotional dyscontrol. |

## *Control of Emotions and Impulses*

I would like to pay special attention to this particular ego function by way of a model developed by Mardi Horowitz and colleagues that is especially useful for understanding the experience of emotions and the resulting impact on personality functioning (Marmar, 1991). According to Horowitz, people respond emotionally in one of three ways: *overcontrol, dyscontrol,* or *emotional tolerance.* (See Figure 13-C.)

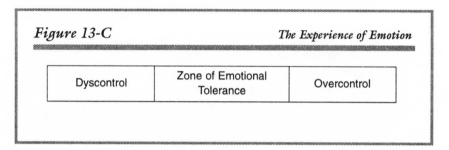

*Figure 13-C*                              *The Experience of Emotion*

| Dyscontrol | Zone of Emotional Tolerance | Overcontrol |
|---|---|---|

*Overcontrol* is a state of mind in which a person either automatically or consciously attempts to ward off the experience of a painful feeling. There may be cognitive acknowledgment of distressing events and some vague, inner awareness of unpleasant emotions. However, in a number of ways, the individual is backing away from experiencing the feelings head-on. Overcontrol is maintained by avoiding situations that potentially could trigger emotions, by using distractions (e.g., excessive involvement in work, keeping active, exercise, and so on), intellectualizing, rationalizing, denial, and minimizing (e.g., "It's no big deal," "Worse things have happened to others," "I can handle it"), or by emotional numbing (either by the abuse of substances or by defense mechanisms such as dissociation).

Overcontrol is a natural, normal way of responding to difficult and painful life events. It can serve adaptively by keeping emotions at bay. Yet it can be carried to extremes and interfere with the processes of mourning and working through painful emotions.

*Dyscontrol,* conversely, is a state of mind in which the individual's defenses seriously fail. The person is overwhelmed by extremely intense emotions or impulses. It is important to emphasize that dyscontrol is much more than just feeling strong emotions. It represents a flood of painful affects that are almost intolerable and can potentially result in severe fragmentation or disorganization of the personality. Most higher-functioning people never experience true dyscontrol, although particular life crises do evoke strong painful feelings. Dyscontrol is almost always seen in the context of ego weakness and severe psychopathology.

*Emotional tolerance* is a state of mind in which a person does, in fact, experience very strong emotions, and yet is able to tolerate the experience. In such instances, the individual may become flooded by sadness, fear, and so on, which certainly may "feel" overwhelming, yet the experience does not lead to disorganization. The individual lives through waves of intense emotion, it passes, and then he or she reenters a less intense state of mind.

As you track moment-to-moment interactions during therapy sessions, you will be able to observe the dynamic ebb and flow between these different emotional states of mind.

Let's illustrate the model with three figures. Figure 13-D shows Mr. A., a high-functioning, emotionally mature man who has recently lost his wife to breast cancer. He has the ego strength to contain most of his inner painful feelings during the day while he works as a general contractor. He is willing and able to speak openly about his emotional frame of mind with his two grown children, however; and he can cry with them when they talk about their loss. At such times, he often experiences intense sadness, but he feels secure enough to

---

*Figure 13-D*                                    *Mr. A.'s Emotional Experience*

| Dyscontrol | Zone of Emotional Tolerance | Overcontrol |
|---|---|---|
|  | With Kids | At Work |

share this sadness with his kids, and almost never feels completely out of control. Often, after talking with his children and weeping, he feels better. His experience is that his strong feelings make sense; he loved his wife, he misses her terribly, and the shared sadness leaves him feeling close to his children. Does he need therapy? Probably not.

In contrast, Mr. B. (see Figure 13-E), who has also lost his wife, has never felt comfortable with strong feelings. He grew up experiencing a significant amount of shame regarding the expression of emotions and has developed a characterological stance that can be described as rigid and overcontrolled. On the rare occasions when he has "broken down," he has felt intense sadness, but never true dyscontrol. In the aftermath of these emotional moments, he felt anxious and a degree of humiliation. He has the capacity to feel his emotions and enough ego strength to tolerate them. But he doesn't trust them and is committed to keeping a lid on his feelings. He doesn't want to "burden" his kids with his strong feelings and prefers to be "strong for them."

| *Figure 13-E* | | *Mr. B.'s Emotional Experience* |
|---|---|---|
| Dyscontrol | Zone of Emotional Tolerance | Overcontrol |
| | Avoid at All Costs | Stay in Control Remain Here |

Should Mr. B. enter psychotherapy, a major goal would be to help him loosen the grip on his extreme defenses and support him in making contact with his inner, truer emotional self. Because he's neurotic, he may be afraid of intense feelings, but ultimately he would find that he could endure them, and real emotional healing could then begin as he more openly mourned his loss.

Finally, Figure 13-F shows Mr. C.'s emotional experience. Mr. C. has also lost his wife. He is a man who has always functioned at a borderline level. His capacity for experiencing strong feelings in an adaptive way is almost nil.

In Figure 13-F we see that Mr. C. has absolutely no zone of emotional tolerance. Thus, he grits his teeth and tries to avoid many sources of stress, especially situations or thoughts that might remind him of his loss and his current state of loneliness. Often, these attempts are unsuccessful and he plunges into a state of extreme despair. He describes such times as "being engulfed in overwhelming blackness and panic." These times are overwhelming and always provoke strong reactions (e.g., on a number of occasions he has flown into rages, breaking furniture and threatening his children).

| *Figure 13-F* | | *Mr. C.'s Emotional Experience* |
|---|---|---|
| Dyscontrol | | Overcontrol |
| Either Here | | Or Here |

Once, he recounted feeling a sudden, intense sense of panic. "I thought I was going to lose my mind. I felt shaky and a strange urge to smash my fist through a window. I dug my fingernails into my arm until I started to bleed. I went to my bedroom, drank a two-liter bottle of wine, and passed out." It is not surprising that he is often plagued with recurring thoughts about suicide.

A psychotherapeutic approach geared to help Mr. C. "get in touch with his feelings" is very likely to push him to dyscontrol, with disastrous consequences. We must first help this man to become more stabilized. The treatment must help him to shore up his faltering defenses and, in general, to improve ego functioning before any attempts are made to explore his intense feelings of sorrow and loss.

This particular model of the experience of emotion can be especially useful for therapists in tracking moment-to-moment experiences in therapy sessions. There is a continuous dynamic ebb and flow as clients talk and shift back and forth among these three main states of affective experiencing. A good deal more is said about the use of this model in later sections of this book.

## *Levels of Interpersonal Relatedness*

This fifth ego function also deserves special consideration. Again, let's consider a continuum. On the healthy end are the individuals who can form intimate connections. Capable of empathy, altruism, and commitment, they are able to establish relationships based on trust, give and take, and they genuinely care about the welfare of the other, independent of their own personal needs.

At the extreme pathological end are people who are either profoundly detached (e.g., severe schizoids) or those who enter relationships only to use or hurt the other (e.g., antisocial personalities; malignant narcissists).

Neurotic-level clients often come to therapy complaining of problems in relationships that include the following: difficulties with intimacy (e.g., feeling inhibited about intimacy, or conversely, having chronic feelings of loneliness and longing for more in important relationships), ambivalence regarding commitment, feelings of jealousy or competitiveness, feeling inadequate in the presence of overpowering people, or experiencing difficulties in clearly communicating with others. However, despite these problems, most neurotic people basically have the desire and the capacity to love others.

For most borderline-level clients, however, interpersonal relations are a source of intense pleasure and pain. Marked egocentricity is a defining characteristic of severe personality disorders. Despite what some of these severely impaired people call "true love" for others, most often the reality is that their relationships are based on "need gratification" (i.e., the central feature is wanting, needing, demanding that "I come first," and that the other exists only to meet their needs). This often translates into a motivation to enter therapy based more on a need to be taken care of than to do the work of personal growth. A predominantly egocentric level of relating can be seen in numerous behaviors, including the following:

- *Very* strong reactions to separation or rejection

- Major difficulties being alone

- Manipulative suicidal gestures in response to interpersonal stresses

- Fits of temper or rage when others do not meet their needs

- A tendency to fall in love quickly or to idealize others, yet rapid shifts into anger or devaluation if others do not meet their needs

- Clinginess, helplessness, neediness

- Difficulties ending therapy sessions on time and the tendency to make multiple calls to therapists between sessions.

Problems in relationships rank among the top sources of psychological suffering seen in our clientele. In addition, the client's capacity to develop some degree of trust in the therapeutic relationship can be a decisive factor affecting either success or failure in brief treatment. Thus our understanding of their level of interpersonal relatedness will be important as we assess what is realistically possible in the course of brief treatment.

## *Summing Up: Ego Functions*

As people encounter difficult times, they must tap into inner adaptive resources (i.e., ego functions) and will have greater or lesser degrees of success in coming to terms with their current life circumstances. The ego functions of thought processes, reality testing, defenses, control of emotions and impulses, and one's level of interpersonal relatedness can serve as markers or barometers for the therapist to assess on an ongoing basis. Aside from reports of subjective distress and particular symptoms, keeping a close watch on the ebbs and flows of ego functions can be a good way to monitor a patient's current state and to track improvement.

## ❖ *Personality Styles*

An appreciation for the varieties of personality style can help therapists better understand their clients' inner, subjective frames of reference. A comprehensive discussion of personality styles is beyond the scope of this book (see Horowitz et al., 1984, for a more detailed discussion). However, I briefly address some features of the most common styles here. Having a clear perspective on these issues can help us more accurately comprehend and empathize with our clients as well as serve as a guide for choosing certain interventions. The dominant features associated with the primary pathological personality styles are outlined in Figure 13-G.

| *Figure 13-G* | Obsessive-Compulsive | Histrionic-Hysterical | Anti-Social | Schizoid-Detached |
|---|---|---|---|---|
| **Areas of particular emotional vulnerability** | Experiencing criticism, failure, loss of control, feeling strong emotions | Interpersonal loss or rejection | Being controlled or dominated by others | Forced interpersonal contact |
| **Cognitive Style** | Analytical, focused, logical rigid | Global, holistic | Varies | Varies |
| **Primary Defenses** | Intellectualization; Rationalization; Isolation of Affect | Pollyanna-denial; Repression | Acting out; externalization of blame | Withdrawal |
| **Emotional experiencing and expression** | Rigid containment and attempts to avoid feelings | Outward expression; often labile | Suppress "soft emotions" (sadness), and act out (e.g. anger) | Emotional blunting |
| **Common stance toward the therapist (and toward others)** | Compliant; seeks advice | Dependent; seeks support | Competitive | Distant, mistrusting |

*Pathological Personality Styles*

*Paranoid individuals have many characteristics that are similar to those seen in obsessional personalities. Two main versions of paranoid style exist: (1) angry-suspicious paranoid and (2) fearful-avoidant paranoid

An appreciation for these issues will help the clinician to understand more about how particular stressors affect each client, what defenses and resistances they are likely to encounter, and what possible factors in the therapist-client relationship to anticipate.

### Signs and Symptoms of Possible Neurobiological Dysfunction

Since psychotropic medication is the treatment of choice for some disorders, and an important adjunct for others, the clinician must be alert to particular signs and symptoms that suggest that a client may benefit from medication.

These disorders and clinical markers are organized below in outline form.

I.  *Strongly consider pharmacological treatment*
    A.  Psychotic symptoms
    B.  Manic symptoms:
        - flight of ideas, pressure of speech
        - psychomotor agitation
        - marked mood swings
        - decreased need for sleep
    C.  Major depressive symptoms (especially when accompanied by the following):
        - sleep disturbance
        - appetite/weight changes
        - anhedonia
        - severe fatigue
        - decreased sex drive
        - severe suicidal impulses
    D.  Disorders that are unlikely to benefit much from brief psychotherapy, but may be helped with psychotropic medications
        - dysthymia
        - generalized anxiety disorder

II.  *Consider pharmacological treatments as an adjunct to brief psychotherapy*
    A.  Depressive disorders of moderate severity
    B.  Acute stress reactions with serious symptoms (e.g., marked insomnia, panic attacks)
    C.  Panic disorder
    D.  Complicated grief reactions (especially if accompanied by the following):
        - severe sleep disturbances
        - marked weight loss
        - agitation
        - anhedonia
        - suicidal ideas

III. *Consider pharmacological treatment as an adjunct to psychotherapy* (although these disorders often may require more lengthy treatment)
  A.  Obsessive-compulsive disorder
  B.  Chronic, severe and/or delayed post-traumatic stress disorder
  C.  Entrenched cases of panic disorder

❖
### Other Client Characteristics That May Be Related to Treatment Planning and Outcome

To round out this section on assessment, let's consider the following issues that often prove to be critical factors in a client's outcome in psychotherapy. These variables are especially important to consider in determining whether or not a particular client is likely to benefit from shorter-term psychotherapy, and will influence one's choice of treatment strategies.

### The Existence of a Focal Problem

Typically when clients are able to identify a particular, or focal, problem, this is predictive of a more successful outcome in brief therapy. This appears to be the case for two reasons. First, people presenting with multiple, severe problems/stressors may simply not be as amenable to brief treatment. Second, the ability for a client to identify and articulate a focal problem, in itself, is often a sign of ego strength. To spell out a concrete problem requires the cognitive ability to conceptualize life events in a fairly clear fashion. An example of this might be, "I have difficulty taking a stand with my husband. I tend to give in a lot, and end up feeling dominated by him." This kind of description stands in sharp contrast to a client who states, "I don't know what's wrong. My whole life is screwed up. I just feel awful and I don't know why."

Certainly we can and do successfully treat many clients that have numerous life problems or are unable to be clear about specific focal issues. To the extent that one can define focal issues, however, there is *generally* a better prognosis for success in brief therapy.

## *Stressors*

Typically, brief therapy is more successful in the treatment of people who have experienced fairly discrete stressors (versus those who present with pervasive, ingrained character problems and an absence of acute stressors). Stressful events generally destabilize people so that even if there are what we consider to be "character problems," we have a better chance of facilitating change, if it is in the wake of recent stressors.

## *Psychological Mindedness*

This refers to the ability and willingness to introspect (i.e., to look inside oneself) and to be aware of inner thoughts, beliefs, sensations, needs, and emotions. Interestingly, this capacity can be independent of one's intellectual level or diagnosis. Some incredibly bright people are virtually unable to introspect. Likewise some high-functioning individuals (e.g., neurotic-level obsessional people) are profoundly cut off from inner experiences, while some quite fragile borderline folks can easily access inner thoughts and emotions. Whether or not a client is psychologically minded has a significant impact on the chosen approach to treatment.

## *The Courage to Face Painful Realities*

Another factor often independent of diagnosis or level of functioning is the courage to face painful emotions and realities. I have been impressed by some of my very wounded, borderline clients, for example, who despite marginal ego strength, have had the willingness to face tremendously painful issues. Conversely, many of our clients are understandably terrified of certain, specific issues or of intense emotional arousal in general. Obviously, the approach and pace of treatment will vary considerably depending on this particular capacity.

## Level of Intellectual Functioning

This must always be considered as therapists choose a particular approach to treatment. Many people are technically within the average range of intelligence, but tend toward very concrete thinking. For these individuals, not only are many therapeutic techniques ineffective, but they ask more of clients than they can do (which can result in the clients feeling inadequate or ashamed). For those people lacking in the capacity for psychological mindedness and/or who tend either to be quite concrete or of lower intelligence, it is essential for the therapist to adjust techniques (as well as language) to meet the client on his or her own level.

## Level of Superego Development

One of the most important predicators of poor outcome in brief treatment is the absence of a relatively well-developed conscience. Those with inadequate superego development often function on a primitive and very egocentric level (with regard to interpersonal relationships). They also tend to externalize blame, and defend by use of acting out and substance abuse. Of course these people are also subject to significant life stressors and can suffer a great deal. However, owing to entrenched character problems, the likelihood of being helped by a course of brief therapy is low. Generally supportive treatment, and a rather directive approach to reality testing and concrete problem-solving are the only interventions that may offer some help to these individuals.

## The Ability and Willingness to "Own" a Problem

This is the capacity to acknowledge one's own role in current problems. This can be illustrated with the following examples: "I know that a part of the reason I am so depressed is because I am very sensitive to criticism, and this demotion at work is hitting me hard," or, "I'm sure that a part of the problem in my marriage is that I get very worried and insecure about our finances, and then I tend to work too much. I know that lately I haven't been as close to my wife as I was during the early part of our relationship."

In contrast are those individuals that are either unable or unwilling to assume responsibility for their predicament. These clients externalize and project blame onto others.

To the extent that a client can "own" his or her problem, brief treatment is more likely to be successful.

## *Finally and Briefly*

The following are also very important in assessing suitability for short term psychotherapy:

- The presence or absence of significant substance abuse
- Sense of humor
- Likability and friendliness
- The presence or absence of an intact, supportive social network (friends, relatives, church, and so on)

## ❖ *Summary*

In a nutshell, these various dimensions of personality functioning can give therapists an initial perspective from which to embark on psychotherapy, and can facilitate our choices of both general and specific strategies.

- *Level of Functioning*
  How sturdy is the client? How aggressive can we be in treatment? What will be a realistic pace? What risks are we taking as we begin treatment? Can brief therapy be helpful?
- *Level of Interpersonal Relatedness*
  Given this issue, what can we anticipate in terms of the client-therapist interaction? How can this inform us about the nature of recurrent problems the client has in relationships?
- *Personality Style Variables*
  What are the likely areas of particular emotional vulnerability? How does this person generally cope with stressful situations (both in terms of defenses employed and characteristic interpersonal stances/maneuvers)? How is he or she likely to perceive and think about things, and how is he or she likely to deal with emotions?
- *Signs of Neurobiological Dysfunction*
  Is the client a candidate for psychotropic medication treatment?
- What *other characteristics* should be noted in assessing potential strengths and liabilities? How will these be related to treatment planning?

**14** ❖

# *Assessing the Nature of Precipitating Events*

Related to assessment is understanding the nature of recent stressors that have propelled a client into treatment. We first consider two important and general aspects of stressful events and then take a look at specific issues that commonly occur in the lives of our clients.

Clearly not all people respond to a similar event exactly the same. At least two variables account for this. The first has to do with the highly unique and personal meaning of an event. As clients are describing life stresses, it is always important to ask, "What is there about this particular event/situation that you found to be especially distressing?" Let's illustrate with an example. A man's wife has decided to divorce him. For one person this event may evoke an underlying schema of "defectiveness" (see Chapter 9). This schema, which may have been dormant, has now become activated and is at the core of his emotional distress. For another man, it may be the prospect of loneliness that disturbs him most (reigniting a latent abandonment schema). In most cases, as we explore the particular aspects of stressful events, it becomes clear that the events have touched on *particular areas of emotional vulnerability* (underlying schemas, a sort of psychological Achilles' heel). People may react to certain stressors (such as a loss) in generic ways, but most often, intensely difficult or painful reactions can be traced to underlying schemas that are being touched on. Understanding the particular issues being evoked is important as we attempt to know our clients' pain.

A second important general issue related to encounters with stressful events is whether or not one experiences a sense of powerlessness versus mastery. When dealing with stressful circumstances, all people (either consciously or tacitly) are taking stock of two issues: (1) the risks and challenges of the stressful events, and (2) an assessment of one's resources (coping skills, emotional endurance, and social support).

Psychologist Albert Bandura (1986) has explored this issue in detail, in studies of what he terms *perceived self-efficacy*. In humans (and in animal studies, as well) when individuals are confronted by difficult, stressful, or painful situations, as long as there is a perception of mastery (e.g., "This is tough, but I can handle it"), the experience may be distressing but not overwhelming. However, when attempts to cope fail and when people begin to conclude that "No matter what I do, I am unable to control or resolve the stress," there is increased risk of emotional collapse. Under these circumstances (referred to by Seligman, 1990, as a state of *learned helplessness*), generally signs of significant physiological arousal are seen to emerge. If this condition persists, often there is an increasing sense of despair, more and more physiological symptoms (such as fatigue, sleep disturbances, and the like), and behavioral inhibition. People often spiral into an increasing state of helplessness, and find it harder and harder to mount effective coping strategies.

It is important to determine how all clients are viewing their current situation, with particular attention to their appraisal of both challenges and their coping resources.

## ❖ *What Has Initiated the Recent Stressors?*

We can delineate seven categories of stressful events, which may have bearing on treatment interventions. These are outlined below.

- Stressors are *random events* that befall the individual (i.e., "fate"). The person has played no role in provoking the events. An example of this would be the sudden death of a loved one.

- Stressors are, at least to some degree, set in motion by the *client's own problematic behavior.* An example is a very dependent person who tends to be exceptionally clingy; this behavior often turns others off, and they pull away. Thus the person's behavior plays a role in provoking repeated interpersonal rejections.

- The stressors appear to be *the stuff of everyday life* (e.g., minor disappointments, or what appear to be slight interpersonal frictions), yet the individual reacts in ways that are clearly exaggerated or otherwise inappropriately intense. In such situations the stressors do play some role in evoking strong reactions, but the exaggerated nature of the person's reaction is largely due to exquisite sensitivity to the particular stressors. This is generally accompanied by a tendency to "take things personally" and/or jump to unwarranted conclusions about even relatively benign interactions or events (this sensitivity may be due to excessive emotional vulnerability and/or constitutional/temperamental factors).

- *Developmental issues* contribute to the emergence of new problems and challenges. Examples: As children grow up and begin to separate from their parents, this may activate feelings of loss in the parent. Decreased physical abilities associated with aging interfere with a valued life activity (such as competitive sports), thus altering a person's life style. Aging parents present new demands on grown children to assume a caretaking role.

- *Loss of a dream:* Often people either in a conscious or an unconscious way have hopes and dreams, for example, the hope that a marriage or a career can be satisfying and meaningful. And in the face of disappointing realities, denial along with hopefulness can distort or obscure the truth for many years. Thus, undesirable situations may be present for a long period of time, yet at some point many individuals begin to see reality more clearly. Denial gives way to more accurate perceptions, and people begin to be hit by the loss of cherished hopes and dreams.

- The *erosion of a support system*. Many people function relatively well in the context of supportive social networks and only experience psychological symptoms when that support is altered or no longer available.

- There may be *no identifiable stressors* (or at least the client can offer none when asked). This may be the case for a number of reasons:

  1. The psychological symptoms may be due to an underlying and possibly unrecognized biological condition (e.g., systemic diseases, hormonal fluctuations [e.g., menopause], endogenous neurological psychiatric illnesses [e.g., bipolar illness].).

  2. The symptoms may be due to the use of medications (prescription or over-the-counter), caffeine, or recreational drugs.

  3. There may be an absence of discrete stressors, but the emotional problems can be traced to the accumulation of numerous smaller sources of stress or chronic, ongoing stressful circumstances.

  4. Stressors have occurred, but have not yet been articulated by the client. (Initially in therapy a surprising number of people are unclear about the role that stressful events have played in creating psychological symptoms. It is only after they begin to take stock of life events during therapy that the picture becomes clearer).

  5. The stressors may not be in awareness for defensive reasons. For example, this is seen in individuals who have experienced significant early-life trauma. Recent events may have triggered or reactivated latent emotional issues. However, in the service of defense, the

client remains oblivious to the meaning of the triggering events.

A basic question we are addressing here is to ask, are the problems and symptomatic responses primarily due to:

- A relatively emotionally healthy person being hit by common stressful events of life?

- A vulnerable person who, in a sense, contributes to his or her own stressors by virtue of maladaptive behavior or exquisite sensitivity?

- A biological disorder affecting brain functioning?

- A mixture of any of the foregoing?

Obviously, our understanding of the client and subsequent treatment planning, goals, and strategies will be influenced by these issues.

### ❖ *Assessing Motivation for Psychotherapy*

To the extent that a client personally wants to enter treatment, and desires some type of personal change, the prognosis is clearly more positive. Unfortunately, a number of people seek treatment for other reasons, including the following:

- Going to therapy because they are coerced into it ("Go to therapy or I'll divorce you!" or going to therapy as a condition of probation).

- Going to therapy to recruit an ally in a struggle against a third party (e.g., to get the therapist to join in bad-mouthing a spouse or to win a custody battle. To have the therapist recommend disability or a leave of absence from work).

- Going to therapy to get drugs (either to abuse or to use to reduce suffering).

Most authors writing about brief therapy have agreed that personal motivation for treatment ranks high among variables influencing outcome (see research done by Sifneos, 1979). And to the extent that a person is suffering, this is often a key to inspiring motivation to enter and participate in therapy ("no pain, no gain"). However, it must also be recognized that although many people are highly motivated to suffer less, this does not necessarily mean that they are motivated to engage in some of the difficult tasks of psychotherapy (e.g., self-disclosure, honestly facing personal shortcomings or intense emotions). All therapists encounter many clients who truly want to hurt less, but are highly motivated to avoid the process of psychotherapy, which can often be emotionally painful and narcissistically wounding.

# 15 ❖

## Assessing the Nature of Psychological Liabilities

We have discussed a number of issues that relate to personality strengths and the processes of emotional growth and healing. At this point, I would like to explore fairly specific *psychological liabilities*. These are critically important areas of functioning that may account for the failure of any given client to come to terms with current life challenges. I would like to suggest that, independent of the specific symptom disorders or diagnoses, these are the issues that should serve as a guide for choosing interventions. In a sense, we are asking about our clients, *"Why isn't life working for them at this point in time?"* Identifying specific psychological liabilities can guide us as to both general and specific treatment interventions.

Several factors often help answer the question, *Why?* These frequently encountered liabilities are interfering with optimal emotional growth or the capacity for emotional healing:

- *Significant privation,* e.g. poverty, poor nutrition, homelessness, debilitating physical limitations

- *Lack of appropriate social supports*

- *Lack of adequate social skills,* e.g., interpersonal communication, conflict resolution, assertiveness, and problem-solving skills

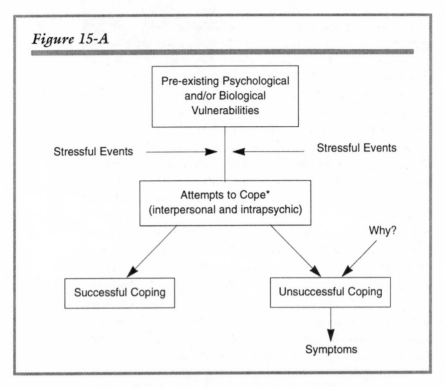

***Figure 15-A***

Pre-existing Psychological
and/or Biological
Vulnerabilities

Stressful Events ⟶    ⟵ Stressful Events

Attempts to Cope*
(interpersonal and intrapsychic)

Why?

Successful Coping

Unsuccessful Coping

Symptoms

\* Will be influenced by a host of strengths and liabilities, e.g., general level of ego functioning, availability of social supports, the adequacy of interpersonal and problem-solving skills, the state of brain functioning, and so on.

- *Factors that may directly interfere with emotional healing processes*

  1. Overdefensiveness

  2. Pain amplifiers: negative cognitions

  3. Negative core schemas

  4. Repetitive maladaptive interpersonal patterns

  5. Underdeveloped or constricted self

  6. Emotional destabilization

- *Factors that contribute to neurobiological vulnerability*

The first three areas on this list obviously can be critical factors that influence the success or failure of people to cope with difficult life circumstances. The first of these represents major social problems — hard realities with no easy answers, and circumstances to address that are well beyond the scope of this book or the wisdom of this author. However, it should be noted that despite what may be tremendous personal strengths and (if available) the best efforts of a skilled therapist, life is an ongoing challenge for many people experiencing these horrendous problems.

In an era of mandated brief therapy, all therapists must come to terms with our limitations. This is a humbling but important thing to acknowledge. At the same time we must give our personal best efforts to provide effective treatment and to tap into any and all existing resources. One such group of resources can be found in many communities: self-help and support groups. The brief therapist should become acquainted with the available groups and, if possible, make a determination about how well they are run. We should often consider these additional sources of support as both an adjunct to psychotherapy and as ongoing sources of support that may extend well beyond the termination of formal therapy.

Finally, let's address briefly the development of coping skills (e.g., communication, assertion, and problem-solving skills). In these areas group experiences can often provide much more than can be realized with individual psychotherapy. In the group context there is the availability of direct learning (lectures, demonstrations, and so on), modeling, role-playing/rehearsal, feedback, and support. This area can also be addressed by way of self-help books. However, as a writer of self-help books myself, I must confess that these approaches are of limited benefit for many people in the throes of significant emotional upheaval. However, self-help approaches may benefit many people confronting certain types of ongoing or long-term difficulties, especially when more acute distress has begun to subside.

Part Four focuses on specific treatment interventions that aim to facilitate change by enhancing our clients' ability to grow and to heal.

## ❖ *Summary*

To complete this section, let's briefly summarize the client variables that predict a greater likelihood of success in brief therapy. We first do this by outlining a "best-case scenario," and then consider complicating factors.

### *Selection Criteria for Brief Therapy*

1. High level of functioning preclinically, and a predominance of "necessary pain"
2. Adequate ego strength (especially the capacity for affect tolerance)
3. Average or above average intelligence and the capacity for abstract thinking
4. Psychological mindedness
5. Ability to articulate a focal problem
6. The presence of recently occurring stressors
7. Some "ownership" of the problem (acknowledging one's own role in current difficulties)
8. Adequate level of superego development
9. Some desire and capacity to relate to others
10. Intact social support system
11. Adequate motivation to participate in psychotherapy.

## Factors Complicating Brief Therapy

1. Characterological problems (very long-term entrenched patterns) predominate
2. Significant indicators of "unnecessary pain" are apparent
3. Tendency toward externalizing blame/responsibility
4. Overreliance on acting out as a primary defense*
5. Significant interpersonal mistrust or detachment*
6. Substance abuse, especially if chronic*
7. Marginal personal motivation for treatment*
8. Ego impairment* (i.e., borderline level of personality functioning)**

* These characteristics represent significant complications and may contraindicate brief treatment.

## Brief Therapy Exclusion Criteria

1. Chronic, severe neuropsychiatric disorders, e.g. bipolar disorder, schizophrenia, dementias, anorexia nervosa, and so on
2. Low-level borderline disorders (manifest by self-mutilation, severe substance abuse, marked emotional instability)
3. Significant antisocial or schizoid features

** For a comprehensive discussion of shorter-term treatment for severe personality disorders, see Preston, 1997.

# PART FOUR

---

# *Targeting Specific Problems: Treatment Strategies*

O nce it is determined that a person is a candidate for brief psychotherapy, we can begin to think about specific approaches to treatment.

In previous chapters we have explored fundamental concepts regarding emotional growth and healing. At the heart of this are three basic assumptions. The first is that a lot of what becomes identified as "pathology" actually represents an individual's best efforts to cope with difficult life circumstances. This implies an inherent desire and attempt to cope and to avoid emotional suffering. Unfortunately, of course, many approaches to psychological coping are ineffective and/or can become a source of additional trouble for people (solutions that backfire). The second assumption is that all people (to a greater or lesser degree) have an inner, inherent striving for growth and emotional health, although this often becomes derailed. And the third assumption is that there is the possibility of change during one's lifetime, which is often facilitated by certain positive interactions with others, psychotherapy being one of them. Psychotherapy can best be seen not as a "curative treatment" (in terms of the medical model), but rather as an interpersonal experience and a set of interventions designed to facilitate emotional healing, personal growth, and more effective coping.

In this section we begin to look at a set of intervention strategies drawn from a number of models of psychotherapy. These approaches are not just a random hodgepodge of techniques. Rather they are major interventions which can address fairly specific problems of many clients coming into psychotherapy. The choice of intervention should always follow from our understanding of the client. It is helpful in each case to consider the four following questions:

**149**

1. Is there any reason to suspect that the problematic behaviors or symptoms are due to a biologically based disorder (neurochemical psychiatric disorder and/or systemic disease)? If so, obviously a referral for medical treatment is in order.

2. Why isn't life working for this person at this time? What are the specific factors that appear to be interfering with efforts to cope, heal, or to grow?

3. Based on the answers to question (2), what can facilitate better psychological functioning with this individual client? Aside from providing a supportive and accepting environment, what will have to happen in therapy to help my client? This can help us formulate *general* treatment strategy.

4. What should I do, as the therapist, in any given moment, to be most helpful to my client? Are there certain behaviors or experiences that call for some type of remark or intervention from me?

# Healthy Folks and Necessary Pain

When emotionally mature people experience life crises, the process of emotional healing is generally straightforward. With a warm and supportive relationship and encouragement to talk, these people take off, relatively unencumbered by significant inhibitions or barriers. Generally, the therapist's empathic presence enables such clients to launch themselves into the various aspects of healing and growth. The predominance of "necessary pain" in these clients is highlighted by the expression of what appear to be understandable and appropriately intense reactions to life events. Also, there is a relative *absence* of the following:

- Harsh self-criticism

- Extreme pessimism

- Excessive defensiveness

Healthy, mature individuals generally do not immediately open up to personal or painful issues when they encounter a stranger (the new therapist). And many emotionally healthy people may not be accustomed to open discussion of very private matters, or they may be experiencing something for the first time (such as intense sadness). However, with these people, trust and openness can develop fairly quickly in the presence of an empathic therapist.

What is helpful for many of these quite healthy individuals is what Greenberg et al. (1993) refer to as *facilitating experiential processing*. In Western culture, even quite emotionally healthy people often tend to rely largely on conceptual processing. The goal of this treatment approach is to increase awareness of certain inner truths (e.g., what I really believe; how I really feel). Greenberg et al. have described this process in detail in their excellent book. Here is a brief outline of the steps in this process:

1. It is first crucial to *establish a sense of safety* in the therapeutic setting, and this is best done by providing a noncritical, nonjudgmental presence with the client. Healthy people will sense if this is sincere and will generally feel safe enough to begin to open up.

2. *Encourage clients to talk* about what most concerns them and in particular to describe what recent events have led to their decision to come to psychotherapy (Greenberg refers to this as encouraging "story telling"). Thus clients begin to share and begin to articulate aloud.

3. Often people give the "short version" of life events, speaking in global generalities and neglecting details. They can be helped if the therapist suggests that they *slow down, take their time,* and *describe more details.*

4. The therapist must be attentive, tracking moment-to-moment behaviors, and be especially alert to certain cues. These include moments either of hesitation or the expression of some affective response (e.g., a slight change in facial expression or tone of voice), which signal that the client has touched on something that has a special meaning or emotional valence. These "choice points" may be opportunities for the therapist to intervene, for example:

> *"I saw an expression come into your eyes just now, Sara. Did you notice that?"*
>
> *"This sounds very important, can you please tell me more."*
>
> *"You mentioned something just now, could you go back to that and elaborate on it?"*

These questions and remarks are designed to help the person share more (in particular, to give more specifics and to explore more deeply what has just happened in the session).

5. Finally, and very important, the therapist inquires in a way to try and understand the personal meanings of thoughts, feelings, and events being shared by the client.

*"You said it upset you. In what way?"*

*"What was there about this encounter that was especially painful for you?"*

Much of the time, the therapist does not intervene. The saying, "Don't just do something, sit there!" is often appropriate, since we do not want to interrupt the client's process. Interventions that are chosen are generally helpful for five purposes:

1. To check out and make sure we are understanding accurately (e.g. "It sounds to me like you are saying thus and so. Am I hearing that right?").

2. To convey our understanding to the client.

3. To draw attention to, highlight, or intensify what we have just witnessed or heard from the client.

4. To flesh out certain issues by encouraging the client to explore in more detail or to take stock of any internal thoughts, emotions, or sensations the client is experiencing.

5. To deal with minor resistances or hesitancies.

With emotionally mature folks, and when the therapeutic relationship is right, you will usually witness outward signs of progress in therapy as revealed in the following changes (Greenberg et al, 1993)

- Decreased hesitancy and increased spontaneity/openness.

- Increased clarity (i.e., a better understanding of what has happened and how one thinks and feels). Emotional reactions begin to make sense and seem understandable.

- Often, a sense of relief.

- Increased self-acceptance.

An accepting and empathic relationship, encouragement to speak, and the interventions noted here, are all that is required to help some clients mobilize their own inner emotional healing resources. Unfortunately, the majority of people coming to psychotherapy exhibit a number of problems that can be seen as roadblocks to healing and growth. These are the *psychological liabilities* outlined in the last chapter. When these obstacles are present, being supportive and showering the client with empathy may feel good, but may simply not suffice to help make something happen. With most clients, we need to be keenly alert to these various liabilities and at appropriate moments, "Don't just sit there; intervene." Being an active therapist is especially important in brief therapy. Often the goal is to help remove obstacles so that the individual may begin to access and to rely on underlying potentials for growth and healing.

**17** ❖

# Major Road Blocks: Dealing with Resistances

Dorothy reluctantly came to her first psychotherapy appointment, having been referred by her physician. "I don't really know why I am here." During the past two months she has been suffering from tension headaches, fitful sleep, and difficulties concentrating while at work. When asked about her current life circumstances, she reported: "Things have been somewhat stressful. A couple of months ago my mother had a stroke, and a lot of my time is spent talking on the phone to her doctors and to the nursing home. My son is worrying me. He's hanging out with a bunch of weird kids and lately he has been talking about getting his nose pierced. And Jim, my husband, and I seem like we are always irritated with one another. Yes, it has been stressful, but I know that this is just a part of ordinary life. Other people have it worse, and it's really not that big a deal. I've been stressed out before and not had these headaches. I really do not think I have a psychological problem."

One of the most common problems people face when trying to come to terms with emotional pain is the tendency to overdefend against the awareness of inner thoughts, needs, and feelings. This can be seen in characterological forms as people navigate through life, massively sealed off from many aspects of their inner selves. It is also seen in response to more recent or acute stressful circumstances. Just as it is natural to reflexively pull a burned finger away from a hot stove, people also quite automatically pull back from awareness of inner painful experiences. Defenses are an absolutely necessary protective mechanism, hardwired into the human psyche. However, if defenses are too

**155**

extreme, pervasive, or chronic, the process can markedly interfere with both emotional healing and the growth of the self. Thus, dealing with resistances in therapy is one of the most important interventions a therapist may employ to bring about change.

As people talk during therapy sessions, what we often hope to see (in those with adequate ego strength) is the expression of at least some spontaneous, real emotions, emotions that are associated with important issues they are thinking about and sharing with us. What one often sees, however, are various ways that people sidestep authentic feelings: hesitancy, avoidance, stilted talk *about* issues but without much affect — a psychological "gritting of the teeth." In these moments we are able to observe the impact of defenses that are operating to keep the person at arm's length from the full intensity and awareness of inner truths. Recall our diagram from Chapter 13 , and let's track a brief example of this phenomenon in a session with Richard. His wife has just left him for another man.

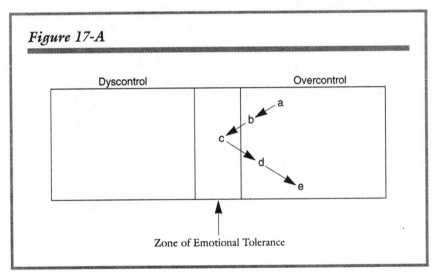

**Figure 17-A**

Dyscontrol

Overcontrol

Zone of Emotional Tolerance

Richard:   *I think about her all the time* [a] *especially at night* (he looks sad) [b] *it's so hard* (his voice cracks) [c] *but I know that others have gone through this kind of thing and survived* [d] *I gotta just get on with my life* [e].

He begins to connect with his feelings, and then we experience a shift. It is likely that this movement away from emotional experiencing was neither conscious nor random. Rather, it was likely motivated by the emerging emotional pain. Like the hot oven, he automatically backed away (by using the defenses of rationalization and intellectualization). In therapy sessions we will see an ongoing shift toward and away from contact with inner emotions.

What Richard did (activating a defense) and what we experienced (sensing the shift in his affect) are what classically have been referred to as *resistances* (resistances are defense mechanisms in action, as experienced at certain moments in therapy).

Resistances have been viewed in a number of ways by various authors. What I present is only one perspective, but certainly one that I advocate. Often therapists experience some type of counterforce. As a client is moving toward what seems to be an important, meaningful awareness, he or she backs away. Affective expression is inhibited (the specific way this is manifest, of course, depends on the particular defenses being used). It may feel akin to cruising down the highway and shifting from fourth into first gear.

As psychologist Murray Meisels has suggested, this often provokes a countertransference reaction in the therapist (feeling frustrated, irritated, or impatient with the client). He further suggests that at the root of the therapist's reaction is often a narcissistic injury: The therapist, confronted with the resistance, feels impotent, humiliated, or a sense of failure. And a common consequence is then to blame the patient, "He is resisting. She is being uncooperative. She is being stubborn!" Meisels offers a different view of this. The client, in this case Richard, has begun to move toward contact with what may be emotionally painful feelings, or material that if revealed would lead to feelings of shame or vulnerability. He backs away and defends, but only after having approached the material. Meisels sees resistance as a phase in the emergence of material into conscious awareness; as a way station (1988).

Here is a metaphor. A boy walks partway out onto a frozen lake, and then becomes concerned that the ice is too thin. Afraid to fall through the ice, he returns to shore. We could choose to focus on his retreat, "Well, he didn't go across the whole lake," or we could view it from another perspective. "He did get scared, he did retreat, but only after he had courageously ventured out onto the frozen lake." This perspective appreciates his progress *and* courage *and* honors his fear and desire for self-protection. All too often resistance is seen in a pejorative light rather than appreciating it as an important phase of treatment and a natural human desire to avoid pain or shame. It bears keeping in mind that *resistances always occur for one reason — the person is afraid.*

Much of early psychoanalytic writing saw resistances as anything that opposed the therapeutic process, and an obstacle to be overcome. Surely excessive defensiveness can result in substantial stunting of growth, interfere with healing, and derail psychotherapy. But it may be more appropriate to see it not as an unfortunate inconvenience, but rather as an important part of human functioning, and a very common experience encountered in most treatment cases. James Bugental offers a neat metaphor: While drivers on a highway react with frustration when they come to a roadblock or detour, highway construction workers see the signs and think "Here is where I go to work" (1995). Likewise, with many if not most of our clients, the resistances we encounter are not an impediment to therapy; they are the therapy. This is where we do our work.

### ❖ Excessive Defensiveness

> *Neurosis is always a substitute for legitimate suffering*
>
> — Carl Jung

Growth and emotional healing can become significantly bogged down in cases where there are excessive resistances. Overdefensiveness in the context of adequate ego functioning is the hallmark of neurosis. These people are so cut off from inner emotions, that working through or mourning is hampered. If the overuse of defenses is long-standing, it often accounts for a stifled sense of self. People are too isolated from inner sources of aliveness and authentic experiencing of life, another characteristic of the constricted neurotic style. Thus, if we identify excessive defensiveness as a major liability, then intervention strategies chosen will aim to lessen the grip of resistance and foster more openness and more inner awareness. It is very important to emphasize, however, that interventions designed to reduce resistance can only be helpful if the following conditions exist:

- If there is an established supportive relationship with the therapist so the client can feel safe (especially from being criticized or shamed).

- If there is adequate ego strength (to reduce or undermine resistances in fragile people can promote decompensation). Many borderline clients have little capacity for tolerating intense emotions, and if defenses fail, they will either experience pronounced dyscontrol and/or will rely on desperate, maladaptive defenses to avoid the underlying emotions (e.g., self-mutilation, severe substance abuse). With these clients, almost always the best approach is to build and strengthen defenses, not to reduce them.

- If the timing is right (i.e., the person is in a place of readiness to be open to inner feelings). The person must be able to feel and tolerate the emotions, and to process the experience, rather than be overwhelmed by it.

As clients explore the edges of their emotional pain, or as we gently probe, we will often see them wince (a moment of emotion and then a pulling back from the pain). This can give us a clue, "Here is where it hurts." It also gives the therapist a direct window into the unique and characteristic ways the person has developed to deal with emotional pain.

Although types of resistance have been described in a number of ways, I would like to outline the most commonly encountered resistances in the next section. Then we will move on to talk about specific strategies for dealing with resistances as they occur.

## *Resistances*

- Most are not under conscious control. They generally occur automatically and without awareness.
- Resistances always occur when clients are beginning to approach material that is either too intense, too painful, or which, if revealed, would lead to feelings of shame and/or vulnerability.
- It is important to make a distinction between the *phenomenon* of resistance (something occurring in the client) and the therapist's *reaction to* the resistance (which may be a countertransference reaction).

### Types of Resistances

The client may be resisting any or all of the following:

- Resistance to change in general (often because what is familiar feels safe).

- Resistance to the *process* of therapy. Most psychotherapy, to a degree, is narcissistically wounding (Michaels, 1990). As people begin to notice their inner emotions more fully, and especially as they begin to share these with the therapist, it can stir up feelings of vulnerability, low self-esteem, and shame. Understandably, many people are reluctant to experience these feelings. (Obviously the stance and general attitude of the therapist are crucial here. To the extent that the relationship can provide tremendous support and freedom from shaming, such resistances may be reduced).

- Resistance to the influence of the therapist. This can have a number of meanings. For some clients, an importantly painful early experience was to be controlled or dominated by powerful others. Thus, for these people, to resist the therapist can actually be seen as a strength or a necessary and understandable interpersonal maneuver. Another very common version of this is seen in people who are attempting to develop a more autonomous self or are protecting what they experience as a tenuous self. Thus the act of resisting the therapist's influence may be appreciated as a form of self-activation. Some resistances may arise out of the client's need to be competitive or from fears of feeling dependent. Finally, transference reactions may set the stage for the need to resist. For example, the reality may be that the therapist is not at all critical or shaming. However, powerful early experiences of being brutally judged and humiliated have set the stage for a client to anticipate such treatment, and to misperceive certain responses from the therapist to be critical or shaming. This prompts defensiveness.

- Last, there is resistance to self-awareness. To become aware of certain inner needs, thoughts, memories, or emotions (the "truth" of inner experiences) may be frightening or very painful, and thus it is avoided.

❖ ## *Commonly Encountered Resistances*

It is not unusual to notice common resistances occurring dozens of times in every session. As we take a look at these, let's consider another metaphor. A woman is slowly moving her hand in a horizontal direction as she approaches the flame of a candle. When she gets close enough to feel the heat, something happens. She moves her hand quickly beyond the flame. What is experienced is not intense pain, but just a momentary and subtle experience of heat (what analysts would call "signal anxiety"). This is also illustrated by our now-familiar diagram (Figure 17-B). What particular resistance is mobilized at point "c" depends largely on the individual client's customary defensive style (often this is related to one's personality style or *DSM* Axis II characteristics).

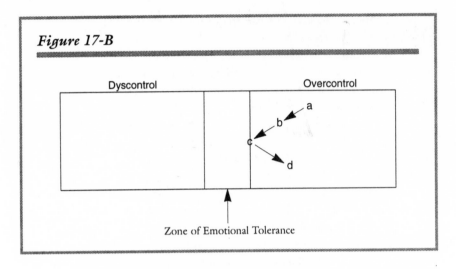

*Figure 17-B*

Now let us consider 16 of the most common resistances.

1. Minimization comments:

> *"I feel kinda angry."*
>
> *"Well, I was probably upset."*
>
> *"Oh, it's no big deal."*
>
> *"It was upsetting, but that's the way life is."*
>
> *"It's over and done with."*
>
> *"I guess I'm sad."*
>
> *"Other people have lived through worse."*

In these examples, an emotion or need is partially acknowledged, but then quickly minimized, reducing the intensity of felt emotion and moving the person back into a state of emotional control.

2. Changing passive to active:

At some level (often unconscious) clients anticipate judgment or criticism, thus instead of passively waiting to be criticized, they become active by being critical toward themselves:

> *"Well, I know this is stupid [silly, ridiculous], but..."*

*"I know this is just making a mountain out of a molehill, but..."*

*Expressing something painful while simultaneously making light of it or laughing at oneself*

3. Critical Injunctions:

*"It does hurt, but I need to be strong."*

*"I don't know why I am feeling this way, it shouldn't bother me so much."*

*"I just gotta stop dwelling on this."*

*"It doesn't help to cry..."*

*"I need to quit being such a damned crybaby."*

4. The therapist points out an affective response that has just occurred, and the client denies it:

Therapist: *Bill, just a moment ago, as you were talking about your Dad's death, I saw a big change come over your face and your eyes got teary. Did you notice that?*

Bill: *Well, maybe, but it's just my allergies acting up. I'm not sad or anything. I got over that a long time ago.*

5. Dissociative symptoms:

This is often manifest by outward signs as well as inner experiences. The client's affect changes. He or she may appear to be dazed; eyes may glaze over. The client often reports feeling an odd emotional or psychological state, often described variously as feeling weird, spacy, mildly confused, or disoriented. There may be a shift in the content of speech as it becomes indistinct, inarticulate, or vague, and often the person feels unclear about what he or she was talking about (there may be amnesia or partial amnesia for what had been transpiring in the moments before the onset of dissociative phenomena).

6. When asked for elaboration or details, the client becomes quite evasive or vague:

Therapist:  *Sherry, you seem pretty upset right now. What's going through your mind?*

Sherry:  *I don't know, I just feel kinda weird.*

Therapist:  *Weird? How do you mean weird?*

Sherry:  *Just odd* (she looks puzzled).

Therapist:  *Well, can you describe your feelings to me in a little more detail?*

Sherry:  *Sure, I guess so. I don't know, I just don't feel right.*

Therapist:  *Yes?*

Sherry:  *You know, I just feel strange, just a very weird kinda feeling.*

Therapist:  *You said you were feeling bad after the meeting with Julie?*

Wayne:  *Yeah, I felt upset.*

Therapist:  *In what way were you upset?*

Wayne:  *I don't know.*

Therapist:  *Well, what feelings did you notice?*

Wayne:  *Just feeling kinda yucky, I guess.*

Therapist:  *Well OK, but yucky in what kind of way?*

Wayne:  *Just not feeling good, just feeling bad.*

Therapist:  *Please tell me what did Julie say that might have rubbed you the wrong way?*

Wayne:  *I don't know, I guess just something about the way she was acting.*

Therapist:  *How was she acting? What, in particular, was she saying or doing that was upsetting?*

Wayne:  *Boy, I just don't know.*

7. Intellectualization and a flight into irrelevant details:

Client:  *I know it's normal for people to be upset, and, all things considered, this has been a difficult time, especially when you consider the number of things in my life lately. For example, like yesterday, I must have spent from three in the afternoon until after eight P.M. worrying about the*

*situation at work, or maybe I even
started thinking about it earlier in the
day, because I know I got home from
church at about one-thirty, so it could
have been even longer than I thought.*

Elaine: *Well, I think this is mainly an existential
issue, certainly not uncommon in lots of
middle aged people.*

Therapist: *Possibly so, but let me ask you, what in
particular were you feeling?*

Elaine: *The closest thing I can come up with is
probably some kind of angst. It's a real
dilemma for managerial level people to find
an appropriate niche.*

8. Moving toward quick closure or "intellectual
insights":

- Previously Ginny had not spoken directly
  about the details of the rape, until today.
  In the past few minutes, she has started to
  talk about some specifics, and begins to
  show outward signs that she is getting in
  touch with some intense, inner feelings.
  Then she says, *"But of course these things
  are upsetting, you know. I probably am
  suffering from a classic case of PTSD. It
  happens a lot with sexual assaults."* (Note
  how the use of the word "it" creates
  further distance from her personal
  emotional experiences).
- Ginny becomes emotional and then states,
  *Oh, it's just that same old childhood
  trauma shit again. I just need to forget it
  and get on with my life!*

Therapist: *John, you seem distressed just now. What's
going on?*

John: *Oh, it's just that mid-life crisis stuff. I'm
just so damned neurotic!*

Therapist: *Well, OK, but what do you mean by that?
What are you aware of?*

> John:  *What I'm aware of is how easy it is for*
> *bright, introspective people to get into*
> *worrying about all kinds of things, and it*
> *makes sense to me. My Dad did it, all my*
> *brothers do it, and I do it too. We are all*
> *screwed up.*

9. The client acknowledges some sensation or
   emotional experience, but is unable to name
   it/label it:
   - *I honestly don't know what I'm feeling.*

10. Emotions are acknowledged, but personal
    ownership is disavowed or denied:
    - *I have been pretty emotional, but it's*
      *probably just PMS.*

> Therapist: *Sounds like you got very angry.*
> Client: *Yeah, I was furious, but that's not the way I*
> *really am. I never get angry. That son-of-a-*
> *bitch pushed me. He made me do it!*

11. Language that negates: Often people make a
    comment that approaches a true, inner feeling,
    only to abruptly negate the experience. This is
    typically done by using the word "but":

    *"I was upset, but it wasn't that big a deal."*

    *"I do miss him, but I'll get over it."*

    *"I did get mad at her, but gosh, she is such a*
    *sweet person."*

    (It has been said that the word "but" stands for
    *B*ehold the *U*nspoken *T*ruth...i.e. the truth of
    what one is willing to acknowledge consciously.

12. Resistance silences: Clearly many silences are not
    born of resistance. Often people are engaging in
    inner reflection, or are searching for words to
    describe inner experiences. However, sometimes
    people say, "There's just nothing on my mind," or
    drift into prolonged periods of silence for reasons
    that are defensive.

13. Using words and phrases that describe experiences
    in generalities, or an abstract way, or language that

otherwise creates distance from inner, more personal experiencing:

- *"That's how a parent is supposed to feel."*
- *"People do get upset."*
- *"These things are difficult."*
- *"It hurts"* (not, "I hurt").

Therapist: *How do you feel?*
Client: *It tends to be a feeling of sadness...*(not "I feel sad").

- *"Well, you know, you feel upset"* (rather than referring to his own feeling).
- Focusing exclusively on what others have said or done, going on and on about factual details of what has happened, while avoiding the mention of any personal feelings or reactions.

14. Clients focus attention on the therapist, rather than talking about their own issues:

*"Well, I'm sure you must have felt this way at times. You do have children, don't you?"*

*"Dr. So-and-So, you look tired today. Are you feeling OK?"*

15. Global conclusions:
*A double-minded man is unstable in all his ways.*
The Bible — James 1, Verse 8

Inner conflict can leave people in a state of dissonance. Thus, one form of defensiveness involves attempts to arrive at firm general, global, or black-and-white conclusions. When the therapist senses that the client may have an assortment of or mixed feelings, a resistance may be inferred.

*The intellect wants a summary meaning, but the soul craves depth of reflection, many layers of meaning, nuances without end...*
— Thomas Moore
*Care of the Soul*

*"I don't know why I'm so upset with my mom. She's basically just a sweet decent person. I guess I'm just screwed up."*

*"I just can't get along with anyone. I'm just a loser."*

16. Flight into health: At a point in treatment when the therapist senses that the client is coming closer and closer to facing something that is emotionally very difficult, the client shows up for the next session reporting that he or she is feeling great. *"For some reason, I've been doing remarkably well this week. In fact, I've even been thinking that I don't really need to come back to therapy for a while. You know Dr. So-and-So, you've been a great help to me."*

These constitute the most common resistances encountered in relatively healthy clients (more pronounced and pernicious resistances are seen with borderline clients and are addressed later in this chapter).

Resistances occur for a variety of legitimate reasons. However, when they are excessive and especially when time-limited therapy is called for, therapists often must take action. We next consider both general and specific strategies for addressing resistances.

❖ *Managing Resistances*
━━━━━━━━━━━━━━━━━━━━━━━━━━━━━━━━━━━━━━━━━━━━

*The absence of fear is not courage.*
*The absence of fear is some kind of brain damage. Courage is the capacity to go ahead inspite of fear and inspite of the pain.*
— Scott Peck, M.D., Author of *The Road Less Traveled*

Timing is critical; we must not challenge or tamper with resistances too early or too aggressively. However, assuming that there is adequate ego strength, a reasonably solid therapeutic alliance, and the time is right, therapists can choose to intervene in such a way as to confront resistances. A critical first step to helping clients to lower their defenses is creating as safe a condition as possible.

In general, we should choose to intervene only occasionally. To jump on every resistance is likely to leave clients feeling badgered, which almost always results in increased, rather than decreased defensiveness. Thus we need to be selective in choosing times to address the resistance.

Mild-level resistances can often be overcome simply by using approaches such as gentle *probing* (e.g., "What are you feeling, Mitch?"), *clarification* (e.g., "Can you please tell me more?") and *confrontation* (e.g., "I just heard some emotion in your voice, Sandy. What do you notice going on in your mind right now?"). These comments and questions can often nudge the person back toward contact with inner emotional experiences. When this does not work or the resistances encountered are stronger, other approaches may be necessary.

The most general strategy is to call attention to the resistance itself. This can be done by inviting our client to examine what has just happened. Let's consider an example. As Joyce began to talk about experiences when she felt ignored by her father as a child (a), her therapist could see a wave of sadness come over her face (b). In the next moment, Joyce said, "But that was so long ago, it really doesn't matter now" (c). The sad facial expression vanished.

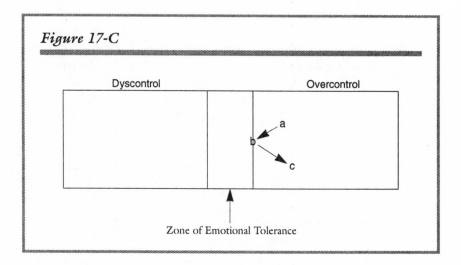

*Figure 17-C*

Dyscontrol                                      Overcontrol

a

b

c

↑
Zone of Emotional Tolerance

*"Joyce, a moment ago you started to look so sad, but when you said, 'It really doesn't matter,' I felt like you moved away from your sadness. Did you notice that too?"*

The therapist is simply flagging the resistance. Note, there is no direct pressure either to feel the emotion or not; the therapist is not passing judgment. He or she is just calling attention to it (or pointing out or demonstrating the resistance). Remarkably, many times this is all that is necessary to break up the resistance (or loosen its grip). Often following such a comment, clients will spontaneously move back into the emotional experience. Sometimes it may require another nudge.

*"How is it right now when you stop and consider the truth of your feelings? How do you feel when you remember those times, Joyce?"*

Here the therapist encourages Joyce to be with herself in the moment and to reflect on her inner experiences. When we intervene in such a way that a resistance is challenged (even if ever so slightly) it is very common to evoke an increase in anxiety or discomfort in our client. Many novice therapists are tempted to back off at this point, but it is important to keep in mind that some increased distress is not necessarily a reason for concern. The client is, of course, entering more difficult emotional territory. In truly low-functioning people, this can represent a danger, but in most neurotic-level clients, the risks are minimal. If the warded-off thoughts or emotions are on the verge of expression, they will unfold. If, however, it's too early or too intense or unsafe, rest assured that most times the therapist will not encounter a tidal wave of emotion, but will witness new defenses immediately coming on line.

## *Suggested Interventions for Dealing with Specific Resistances*

❖

Let's revisit the list of 16 common resistances, and offer some examples of particular interventions that are often effective (T = therapist, C = client).

### 1. Minimization:

    C:  *I feel kinda angry.*
    T:  *Kinda angry?*
    C:  *Well, actually, I am angry.*

    C:  *Well, I was probably upset.*
    T:  *Probably?*
    C:  *Well, somewhat upset.*
    T:  *Somewhat.*
    C:  *No, real upset!*

    C:  *Oh, it's no big deal.*
    T:  *Really? No big deal? Karen, given what you have told me about this and how much it means to you, it's hard to imagine that it's truly no big deal.*
    C:  *Well, it is a big deal to me; maybe not to him, but it certainly is to me!*

    C:  *It's over and done with.*
    T:  *Well, it is over, but please tell me, Beth, in your heart of hearts, does it really feel as if it's completely over?*

### 2. Changing passive to active:

    C:  *Well, I know this is silly but I felt really humiliated.*
    T:  *You say it's silly, but Jim, it seems to me that it did in fact feel very humiliating for you.*
    C:  *Well, to be honest, it did and, I do feel awful.*

    T:  *You said "this is stupid, but..." and then went on to talk about something that was very painful. I'd like to ask you Stan, were you concerned about how I'd react or what I might think?*

C: *I guess I was.*

T: *Please tell me something. You had just told me about something very personal and very painful. How would it have been if I had reacted in some way that made it look as if I thought you were stupid?*

C: *I would have been devastated.*

T: (could choose one of two pathways):

  1. *"Has it been your experience with others in the past, that if you revealed personal things, they would react like you were being stupid?"*

  2. *"Please tell me, in the past few moments what have you noticed about my reaction and how it is to share these feelings with me?"*

C: (laughs as she saying something painful about herself)

T: *Well, I see you chuckling and kind of making light of this, but it seems to me that it's obviously not funny at all. I think what you are sharing with me sounds tremendously painful.*

### 3. Critical injunctions:

C: *It does hurt, but I need to be strong.*

T: *Maybe it has been important for you to be strong, Vince, and I can appreciate that. At the same time, please tell me, how do you feel just now? What do you notice?*
(This intervention acknowledges and accepts the injunction, at least somewhat, but the therapist immediately returns to the emotions of the moment and inquires.)

### 4. Denial of confronted affective reactions:

T: *I just saw a big change come over your face and tears come to your eyes. Did you notice that?*

C: *Well, maybe, but it's just my allergies acting up. I'm not sad or anything. I got over that a long time ago.*

T: *Maybe so; at the same time, we were talking about your Dad's death. When you spoke to me a minute ago about the last time you saw him, what did you notice going through yourself? Take a moment and reflect on this. What are the feelings you notice?*

## 5. Dissociative symptoms:

- Generally dissociative phenomena occur when people who have been very traumatized are beginning to approach underlying frightening feelings or memories. In many respects, I believe, we should respect this defense and only probe cautiously, not wanting therapy to be retraumatizing by dredging up intense material prematurely. Dissociative symptoms often not only block awareness, but also produce subjective experiences that in themselves can be distressing. In such moments many people think that they are going crazy, owing to the weird nature of the symptoms. When this is the case, it can be helpful to give the client a minilecture about dissociation, explaining it as a fairly common human reaction that occurs when people experience very frightening events (in reality or in memory). It is like a neuorchemical version of Novocain, which clouds awareness and numbs emotional pain.

- If the person is solid enough, then the therapist may wish to go back over the topic discussed just prior to the emergence of dissociative signs, checking to see if the client is able and willing to reapproach the material. If dissociation continues or becomes more pronounced, it is a good idea to leave well-enough alone, and for the

time being to back away from the particular
issue being addressed.

### 6. Vagueness:

A general approach to dealing with excessive
vagueness is to include the following steps:

- Ponder aloud, about the possibility that the
  discussion is emotionally difficult for the client
  (acknowledge and empathize).
- Backtrack (rewind the tape) and go to the
  beginning of an event the client has been
  speaking about. Slow him or her down. Ask for a
  lot of details about both the external event and
  his or her own, moment-to-moment reactions.
- As the client offers some details, inquire about
  any feelings, physical sensations, internal self-
  talk, or images he or she is experiencing in the
  moment while speaking to you.
- Call to the client's attention (confront) affective
  cues that you notice as he or she speaks.

### 7. Intellectualization and flight into details:

- Conscious awareness (and experiential
  processing) is most likely when a person has
  access to three realms of experiencing;
  thoughts (or words), emotions, and
  physiological sensations. People who
  overintellectualize are generally operating
  almost exclusively from the arena of thoughts,
  and are almost cut off from emotions. To deal
  with overintellectualization, it is first important
  to be accepting of their style and show a
  willingness to understand things from this
  perspective. As this occurs, three interventions
  may be helpful in redirecting their awareness
  toward other inner experiences;
  a. Encourage the awareness of physical
     sensations (e.g., muscle tension, visceral
     reactions, etc.). Overintellectualizers often
     can, if encouraged, become aware of
     physical sensations (usually much more
     readily than noticing emotions). Have them

describe in detail any physical sensations, in and of itself; this can direct them into another sphere of awareness. It can also promote a shift away from the log-jam of details into a different mode of experience. In addition, as they are able to spend a moment noticing and describing sensation, the therapist can inquire:

*"What do you make of that?"*

*"How does that feel?"*

*"Are you aware of any emotion that goes hand-in-hand with that sensation?"*

*"Have you ever noticed times in the past when you had this same feeling of a lump in your throat?"*

The focus on sensations can serve as a bridge, as it moves the client in the direction of more experiential awareness.

b. Point out affective cues and encourage clients to stop talking and simply notice the physical aspects of emotion. They may spontaneously acknowledge some aspect of emotion, or the therapist may have to inquire, "What's going on and what do you make of that?"

c. A third intervention is not designed to reduce resistance in the moment, but over a period of time it can be helpful. This approach aims at helping the overintellectualizer to live in and notice more of his or her body. It can be accomplished by teaching clients relaxation or breathing techniques, or encouraging them to get involved in certain activities outside of therapy such as stretching, physical exercise, dance, or massage. A secondary outcome may be more relaxation, but the primary goal is to teach them to develop the ability to pay attention to perceive bodily sensations more accurately. As this capacity is developed, there is often a gradual change in clients' awareness of inner emotions (all of which certainly have somatic aspects).

### 8. Quick closure and intellectual insights:

- An approach to this kind of resistance that often is very helpful is to *reframe* what has been said by referring to what you know have been emotional realities from the person's life.

    C: *This is just so upsetting, but I don't know why I let it get to me so much. I guess I'm just too sensitive.*

    T: *I want to ask you something, OK? You have told me a number of times before how much this relationship has meant to you, how important it has been to have a family and to feel a part of Dave's life, right?*

    C: *Yes.*

    T: *You tell me, especially since it has meant so much to you, is it understandable that you'd have strong feelings about the divorce?*

    C: *I guess when you put it that way, it does.*

- Another approach is, once again, to highlight the resistance, and call it to the client's attention.

    C: (almost becomes tearful as he speaks about his divorce) *Look, these things happen. People go through divorces all the time and get over it. I'm sure I will too.*

    T: *Probably so; at the same time, it seems clear to me that you aren't 'over it' yet, and Chuck, even though you say people go through divorces all the time — that's a pretty general statement. We're talking about your life. Let's go back a minute or two, OK? I think you were starting to feel some strong feelings as you were talking about the day Donna told you she was leaving. Could you say more about that?*

    C: *OK, sure.*

(Also note how Chuck says, "...people go through divorces.." — how the resistance puts the experience into the abstract — rather than saying, "I am going through a divorce.")

**9. Unable to label:**

- Recall from Chapters 5 and 10 that difficulty in articulating inner experiences may arise for many reasons, not just resistances. Thus, it is important to try to determine if this phenomenon is born of defensiveness. When clients are hard pressed to come up with any words to express inner feelings or sensations, several interventions may be useful.

  a. Often it is productive simply to tell clients, "Just take your time." This both gives encouragement for them to reflect, and implicitly says, "Maybe it's just natural that it takes a while to look inside and to introspect, and I am in no hurry."

  b. Ask them if they notice any bodily sensations that accompany the feeling (to use this as a bridge to awareness).

  c. Ask them to recall any past times where they experienced something similar, and if so, to explore that situation some, to see if this will bring a clearer understanding to the current moment.

  d. Ask them to tune into the feeling, close their eyes, and visualize, see if any images come to mind

  e. Finally, and only if other efforts fail, the therapist may choose to share his or her own impressions of what is being experienced based on observations of affect and the content of the material being discussed. This should always be presented in a tentative way.

**10. Disavowal of responsibility or "ownership":**

  C: *I have been pretty emotional, but it's just PMS.* (Of course, hormonal changes can

and do influence emotions, but let's
assume, it is likely that this is a resistance.)

T: *You might be right, but nevertheless, how did
you feel?*

C: *I never get angry. That son-of-a-bitch pushed
me; he made me do it!*

T: *Well, probably so. All the same, how was it for
you to feel so upset?*

## 11. Language that negates:

C: *I was upset, but it wasn't that big a deal.*

T: *You say it wasn't a big deal; however, please
tell me, when you look at the impact of this
event, and the strong feelings you have,
would you say it is trivial?*

C: *I do miss him, but I'll get over it.*

T: *I suspect the loss won't be as painful sometime
in the future, however, I believe you when you
say that you do, in fact, really miss him.*

C: *I did get mad at her, but gosh, she is such a
sweet person.*

T: *So she is a sweet person, and you felt mad at
her too.*

This last example deserves some discussion. Many
times people try to arrive at a single conclusion or
view of things (as discussed with resistance #14).
Often this may be seen as an attempt to reduce
complexity or ambiguity in situations. However,
when in fact there are mixed feelings or conflicting
beliefs, to arrive at one conclusion can serve to
restrict awareness (and thus may be seen as a form
of resistance).

## 12. Resistive silences:

Three approaches are often effective:

a. Ask clients if their silence may be due to
feeling distressed or uneasy about what they
have been speaking about. In particular, it

may be helpful to inquire regarding any worries or fears they may be having concerning how the therapist is feeling or what the therapist is thinking.

b.  Explore the precursors to the silence, to try and understand what may have led to the silence.

c.  Tell the client, "If there is something that you are feeling uneasy about discussing, it's really OK with me for us not to talk about it. It's entirely up to you." In other words, you are showing an acceptance that the client may need to be silent or distant.

## 13. Language that creates distance:

C:  *That's how a parent is supposed to feel, right?*

T:  *You are talking about a parent. What I'd like to know is how you feel.*

C:  *These things are difficult (or "It hurts").*

T:  *John, you said it hurts. When you say it, what are you referring to? How are you hurting?*

T:  *How was it to feel ignored?*

C:  *You know, you are uncomfortable and tense.*

T:  *Jeff, you said "you are uncomfortable."*

C:  *Well, I mean, I was uncomfortable.*

## 14. Focusing on the therapist:

C:  *Dr. So-and-So, you look tired today. Are you feeling OK?*

T:  *I am feeling tired, but Jean, what I'd rather focus on is how you are doing.*

C:  *There's a lot of flu bugs going around. You know you really need to take care of yourself.*

Of course this last comment could have any number of meanings (e.g., might she be worried about the therapist's getting sick and then being unavailable? Might this reflect a characterological pattern of putting others' needs before hers?). But let's assume that in this case it is a resistance, and

further let's assume there is a well-established
therapeutic alliance.

T: *Jean, have you noticed that there are times when*
   *you tend to focus on me and my well-being,*
   *rather than talk about yourself?*

C: *I guess so, at times.*

T: *Please understand that I appreciate your*
   *concern; at the same time, however, I wonder if*
   *a part of this is because you may be wanting to*
   *avoid really looking closely at yourself. In our*
   *last session you were getting very close to opening*
   *up about your feelings of sadness about your*
   *mother's death.*

C: *Probably so. Yeah, you're right* (she becomes
   tearful).

## 15. Global conclusions:

- In the following example, Donnie is a
  21-year-old college student.

Donnie: *I was talking with my mother on the phone*
        *last night, trying to tell her about breaking*
        *up with Shelley. By the time I got off the*
        *phone, I felt terrible. I don't know, I just*
        *have a hard time getting along with my*
        *mom. Other people seem to have a good*
        *connection with their parents. What the hell*
        *is wrong with me?*

A part of what we see in this example is how his
conclusion (implying that there is something
wrong with him) accentuates his sense of personal
inadequacy. This may be an example of a
cognitive distortion that is consistent with an
underlying negative schema. Beyond this,
however, it may also be a resistance; a resistance
to awareness of other conclusions, perceptions,
and emotions. Let's see what happens.

Donnie's therapist asked him to tell the story
again, but to give more specifics. Donnie
responded, "There's not much more to say. I felt

lousy after the call, and that's that" (quick closure).

Therapist: *It sounds as though you felt really disappointed after talking with your mom.*

Donnie: *Right.*

Therapist: *I'd like to ask you to tell me about it again, but this time, slow down, take your time. Share with me some more details, OK?*

Donnie: *Uh, OK...(long pause). I said to her that Shelley had just told me she'd gone out with another guy, and it just tore me up to hear that.*

Therapist: *What did your mom say to you then?*

Donnie: *(pause) She said, "Well, son, these things happen. You'll get over it." And then she sorta changed the subject (pause). "I guess she's right."*

Therapist: *Well, maybe, but I want to ask you, at that moment when she said "these things happen," how did you feel? What did you notice in that moment?*

Donnie: *(pause) I felt real let down, real sad.*

Therapist: *Why do you think? What was it in her words that might have touched on that feeling with you?*

Donnie: *I was calling to get support. I wanted her to know how upset and sad I've been.*

Therapist: *You wanted her to be there for you.*

Donnie: *Yeah, and this has happened before with her. She just doesn't listen. Oh, she says she cares, but sometimes I wonder.*

Therapist: *You were reaching out to her and telling her about your feelings, and she didn't really hear you?*

Donnie: *Not at all. She was acting like it was no big deal, but it is a big deal! This is probably the worst time of my life and she doesn't get it!*

Therapist: *You said at the end of the phone call you thought, "What the hell is wrong with me?" What are you thinking now?*

Donnie: *I don't think there's anything actually wrong*

*with me, I think I was mostly upset because*
*she didn't seem to hear me, or to care.*

The outcome has not only reduced defenses and increased his awareness of inner feelings toward his mother. It has also resulted in a clearer and more accurate view of what happened. In addition, it has promoted a shift in his self-perception. He has moved from, "Something is wrong with me" to, "I am a person who is suffering from a loss and experiencing sadness," and "It's understandable at a time like this for a person to want to find support from others." As we discuss in Chapter 19, repeated experiences in therapy, like this example, are one way to begin to alter underlying negative self-schemas.

16. **Flight into health:**
   - I recommend a fairly direct and honest discussion with the client in which the therapist puts forth the possibility that this is a resistance. For example:

     T:  *Sue, I am glad you are feeling better. I do,*
     *however, want to share one thought with you.*
     *Last time we met, it seemed clear to me that*
     *you were on the verge of experiencing some*
     *very painful feelings and memories about the*
     *death of your sister. I can't be sure about this,*
     *but I wonder if in some way those memories*
     *are so painful that your mind pushed them*
     *down deep inside, so much so that you have*
     *been genuinely feeling very good this week.*
     *The point I want to make is that it's possible*
     *that your feeling better may not be the whole*
     *story; maybe there's still a lot of unfinished*
     *business in the back of your mind. What do*
     *you think?*

   - If clients insist that they are, in fact, OK, and want to stop therapy, it is important to say something to make it easy for them to return, should the issues resurface. Once a person has insisted "I'm OK!" he or she may

feel ashamed or otherwise reluctant to
return, if several weeks down the road, he or
she realizes the termination was premature.

T:  *I absolutely believe that it is your decision*
*about whether to stop therapy or not.*
*However, if for any reason you want to come*
*back, at any time, please don't hesitate to call*
*me, OK?*

## ❖ *Common Errors in Managing Resistances*

There are four very common errors all therapists make
from time to time as we deal with resistances.

1. Assuming there is a resistance, when in fact there
   is none (we may be simply misunderstanding what
   is happening, e.g., assuming silence is defensive
   when in fact the person is needing time to ponder
   and process).

2. Moving in too quickly or too aggressively. We
   need to be prepared to back off, to help the client
   restabilize, and, if appropriate, to apologize for
   our error.

3. Sometimes, the client's resistance is dealt with,
   and she responds with noticeable uneasiness. The
   therapist, worried about harming the client, quickly
   backs off. Often, it is important to hang in there
   and be persistent, despite some amount of distress.
   This is the case when we know with certainty (a)
   that the therapeutic alliance is solid (and the client
   knows that we genuinely care), (b) that despite the
   emotional pain, the client has good ego strength,
   and (c) that the timing is right, and not to persist
   would be to collude with defenses and keep
   treatment at a stalemate (a particular problem
   often encountered in brief therapy when the clock
   is always running and time is short). Let's take a
   look at a vignette. It must be emphasized that the
   very persistent approach taken with Mary is only
   occurring because she is strong, the alliance is well
   developed, she is suffering a lot, and she only has
   seven sessions left in a mandated course of brief
   therapy.

Here is her story. She is a 55-year-old widow. Her husband, Ben, died six months ago. Her initial grief had taken a turn for the worse; she has developed a major depression (with current symptoms of marked sleep disturbance, anhedonia, weight loss, severe tension headaches, and suicidal ideas). Throughout treatment she has been significantly overdefended. She is now in her thirteenth session.

Mary: *In the last months before Ben died I just feel like I was a bad wife* (looks away, holding back tears).

Therapist: *How do you feel right now, Mary?*

Mary: *Well, sad, of course* (continues to avoid eye contact). *That's how a wife is supposed to feel when her husband dies. Right?*

Therapist: *You are saying that's how a wife is supposed to feel...I want to know how you feel.*

Mary: (Becomes tearful) *Crying doesn't help. Why should I cry? He's dead; that's just the way it is.*

Therapist: *I wonder if when you say "that's just the way it is" it's a way you keep yourself away from your feelings, and you keep me away from your feelings?*

Mary: *I don't know* (starts to sob, then stops herself). *I just have to get on with my life; I've got so much to do* (she breaks eye contact, and looks tense and stoic).

Therapist: *Just a moment ago when you started to cry, you stopped yourself. How come?*

Mary: *People don't want to hear. They don't want to see a person cry.*

Therapist: *People you know do not want to see that you are sad?*

Mary: *Yes.*

Therapist: *Mary, is it possible that you were thinking that here with me a moment ago?*

Mary: *Maybe I was, I don't know.*

Therapist: *What happens when others see you cry?*

Mary: *They say, "Oh, everything will be all right. You'll get over it!"*

Therapist: *Is that true? Do you think everything will be all right?*

Mary: *No!* (tearful). *My husband was the only one who could really understand me* (begins to sob openly). *I just miss him so much.*

For Mary, this session was a turning point, as she began to open up to her inner sorrow and loneliness. But let's be clear. The therapist, in this vignette, was very persistent. Such an approach could have disastrous effects if the alliance were marginal and if Mary were not truly in a place to face her pain.

Let's look at one more vignette that also illustrates how persistence is often required. This example also illustrates how second-line resistances come on the scene as the therapist confronts them.

Sally: *I guess I'm just under a lot of stress. Some people handle stress better than others do, like the other night we were just watching a TV show, and for no reason, I started to cry. I mean, really cry.*

Therapist: *What was there about the show that touched on these feelings?*

Sally: (Starts to cry, turns head away, breaks eye contact and cries as she shakes her head "no") *It's just so stupid.*

Therapist: *What's stupid?*

Sally: *This old stuff again. It's over with. I should be over it!* (tearful).

Therapist: *Right now it hurts. Things did happen a long time ago and it hurts now.*

Sally: *People get over worse things. What's wrong with me?*

Therapist: *You said, "It's stupid, and I should be over it, and it hurts," you hurt now.*

Sally: *It just hurts so much to remember* (very tearful).

Therapist: *I believe you.*

To bail out too quickly with Mary or Sally would likely have prolonged therapy, or worse yet, may have created such a defensive stalemate that they would get to the end of brief therapy and still be suffering.

4. The last common mistake is to err in the opposite direction. I would like to quote from Jane Thorbeck (1993):

*[the therapist]...feels his or her patient is someone who is more psychologically able, more developmentally mature than the patient actually is. This type of error is particularly common with patients whose apparently competent exterior covers a more vulnerable core, easily misleading the therapist. These are patients who look better on the outside than they are on the inside. The doctor then in his or her own mind holds the patient responsible for a higher level of development than the patient is capable of. To put it simply, the doctor expects more than the patient can deliver.*

This is seen to occur most commonly in clients with an underlying severe personality disorder, or people suffering from significant trauma (e.g., PTSD). To move in and pursue resistances too aggressively can cause marked destabilization. The impact of such an error may be seen during the session, as the client collapses into a state of dyscontrol. Even more commonly, the client leaves the session and either decompensates, or turns to severe acting out (marked substance abuse, suicidal gestures, or self-mutilation). Often clients will drop out of treatment.

Resistances in vulnerable clients are to be respected and not dismantled. But able therapists will, from time to time, encounter the kind of clients described by Dr. Thorbeck. In such cases, we must be quick to act and provide interventions that aim to reinstate defensive controls and help our clients stabilize.

## *Pernicious Resistances*

The following resitstances are not discussed in detail, but are important to mention. When these are a dominant part of the clinical picture, successful treatment with brief psychotherapy may not be possible.

- *"Negative Therapeutic Reaction."* A type of transference reaction where the client is suffering and clearly asks for help, but is tremendously resistant to any and all attempts on the part of the therapist to be helpful. This dynamic is felt to occur because a crucial underlying (often unconscious) motive is for the patient to defeat the therapist (make him/her feel impotent or humiliated). This is hypothesized to occur in some clients with personality disorders who experienced very severe abuse when young. The current in-treatment behavior may serve to punish people in parental or help-provider roles.
- *An Intense Need to Suffer.* Despite pleas for help, some people (consciously or unconsciously) are driven by a need to suffer. This can be seen in the context of severe depressive disorders, and also can be a feature of certain character pathology (intensely guilt-ridden people or those with so-called "masochistic personalities").
- *Severe Acting Out.* Violence and aggression towards others, rampant sexual promiscuity, severe substance abuse, some forms of bulimia, self-mutilation, and so on. Such people almost always have borderline or psychotic disorders, and may not be amenable to brief therapy.
- *Secondary Gain.* If this is pronounced, successful treatment may come to a halt. Lots of people genuinely suffer, yet there may also be significant motivations (conscious an unconscious) to remain ill or dysfunctional. One common example is where a couple is staying together *only* because the husband is afraid if he leaves, his fragile and depressed wife will commit suicide. For her to benefit from treatment may reduce her fragility and symptomatology, and thus ultimately threaten her (admittedly quite tenuous) relationship. The need to maintain attachment may be stronger than her need to recover from the depression. Many people do come to therapy with secondary gain as one aspect of the clinical picture. Often this can be resolved and they can benefit from brief treatment. However, if the secondary gain is powerful and entrenched, it can derail any real movement toward growth and healing.

## ❖ *Summary*

People come to therapy seeking help to promote coping, healing, and personal growth. We have assumed that several experiences are central to the emotional healing process — emotional expression, articulating inner feelings and thoughts, clearly facing difficult realities, and sharing the pain with another. One very common stumbling block to healing is when this process becomes mired in resistances. The client has his or her particular *pain*, but the *problem* we commonly encounter lies in excessive defensiveness. Thus, what we are diagnosing is the nature of any and all *psychological liabilities* that we judge to be interfering with the client's best efforts to cope and to heal. Assuming the client has adequate ego strength, we can choose periodically to intervene, to focus on this particular class of psychological liabilities. *Managing resistances* is when we "go to work" to remove roadblocks, to free up and expand internal experiencing, and, when the time is right, to step back and watch our clients move ahead along the pathway of healing.

# Misery Amplifiers and Unnecessary Pain

Chuck just received the news that he failed his bar exam for the second time. In addition to an intense feeling of disappointment, he has been flooded with a host of upsetting thoughts, "What the hell is wrong with me. I'm just a god-damned loser. I can't believe that I could be so stupid. I'm never going to be able to practice law!"

Unrealistic, negative cognitions are another frequently encountered set of psychological liabilities. These patterns of perception and thinking have two features in common: (1) They involve some distortion of reality, and (2) they operate to turn up the volume significantly on emotional distress. The impact of negative cognitions accounts for the majority of "unnecessary pain." In this chapter we focus on such cognitions as they contribute to two critical areas of emotional suffering — excessive self-criticism and the perception of powerlessness.

### ❖ Ruthless Self-Criticism

*"What the hell is wrong with me?"*

*"I'm so screwed up!"*

*"Why am I so overly sensitive?"*

These, and similar statements, are frequently heard, especially in early sessions of psychotherapy. In the wake of very difficult and painful life experiences, it is amazing how often many (if not most) people entering psychotherapy "sign in" with comments that clearly reveal significant self-criticism (and at times, self-hatred). This source of personal suffering is ubiquitous.

A good deal of this phenomenon can be understood as either a manifestation of chronic attitudes toward the self or as a reactivation of underlying negative self-schemas. At times it can be appreciated as a form of attack on the self, anger directed toward oneself for either exhibiting dystonic emotions (like vulnerability) or for failing to cope well with life circumstances. Such attacks on the self interfere with healing in at least two ways. First, ruthless self-criticism becomes a source of significant emotional pain in and of itself (apart from other events that may have provoked the most recent emotional crisis). Second, focusing on feelings of inadequacy, worthlessness, and the like can distract people from dealing more directly with current sources of "necessary pain." Thus, when we observe an excessive amount of self-criticism, we can flag this as a psychological liability, and choose interventions to address it, three classes of which we address here.

### ❖ Challenging Cognitive Distortions

Often, statements that are self-critical contain inaccurate, global, or arbitrary conclusions. A commonly used intervention is to actively confront what appear to be such cognitive distortions and encourage the client to "explore the facts." However, it must be emphasized that such interventions often initially fail because of one frequent error — hastiness. Most people are not open to this type of intervention until they first feel truly heard and understood. To challenge cognitions too early carries the risk that the client will feel that the therapist either just "doesn't get it" or that the therapist is being critical. However, in the context of a good therapeutic alliance and empathy, and when the timing is right, the therapist can choose to intervene. Let's consider some examples:

> Debbie: *I went to this professional meeting last night and, contrary to my usual style, I decided to speak out. And after I did, this guy looked*

*at me like I was totally stupid. I left the
meeting and ever since then I've felt
terrible.* (She becomes tearful.)

Therapist: *What has been going through your mind?*

Debbie: *That I looked foolish, and everyone there
probably thinks I'm some kind of dumb
bimbo, and I just feel humiliated.* (Note:
"everyone probably thinks" may be an
arbitrary and overly global conclusion.)

Therapist: *It sounds like it was very uncomfortable.*

Debbie: *Yes.*

Therapist: *Debbie, let me ask you something, OK? You
tell me, aside from the one man's reaction,
if you just look closely at the comment you
made in the meeting, in your own opinion,
what do you think about what you said?*

Debbie: *Well, actually, I thought it was a valid
point, but I don't think anyone else
agreed...*

Therapist: *Maybe not; however, I want to ask you to
consider the situation very carefully. The
guy across from you did seem to react in a
negative way, but how about the others? Is
there any clear evidence that everyone
disagreed?*

Debbie: *Well, no, I'm not sure. I guess I felt like I
was on the spot and I felt anxious, and the
jerk across the table obviously didn't like
what I was saying.*

Therapist: *It was risky for you to speak out. I know
that's something you haven't been
comfortable doing. Again, let me ask you —
how about the others?*

Debbie: *No one really criticized me. Actually one
woman came up later and kinda gave me a
pat on the back.*

Therapist: *And, again, based on your own, personal
opinion, did you think your comment had
merit?*

Debbie: *Yes, I do.*

Therapist: *Then would it be accurate to say that it did
feel uncomfortable, when the guy reacted the*

> *way he did, that the two of you probably*
> *didn't see eye-to-eye, and at the same time,*
> *there was some support for what you said*
> *and furthermore, you do believe that your*
> *ideas had merit?*

Debbie: *Yes, that's accurate.*

The goal is not to talk her out of her feelings or to gloss over those aspects of her experience that were clearly unpleasant. But the challenge is to help her more accurately evaluate the whole picture.

Let's consider one additional example. The client is upset following an argument with his wife:

> Client: *I can't do anything right. Everything I*
> *touch turns to shit.*

> Therapist: *Look, I know you are really upset about the*
> *blowup with Kathy. It makes sense that it*
> *would upset you. At the same time, think*
> *for a minute — is it one hundred percent*
> *accurate that you don't do anything right?*
> *What about last weekend when you guys did*
> *a great job resolving your differences of*
> *opinion. Yeah, this last episode was intense,*
> and *there clearly have been times recently*
> *when you've tackled a tough situation and*
> *made it work.*

## Reframing

This approach attempts to offer a new perspective for understanding one's feelings, needs, or reactions, especially by encouraging the client to view things from a broader perspective. The goal is twofold: first, to help move the person to a perspective of greater self-acceptance and self-compassion, and second, to reduce affective intensity by countering the tendency to think or say, "It shouldn't be that way!" or, "I shouldn't feel this way!"

> Client: *I am so completely overwhelmed with sadness, I*
> *can't stand it. What the hell is wrong with*
> *me? I'm so screwed up.*

> Therapist: *Barbara, I want to ask you something. You*

and I both know that you went through a lot
of hell when you were a kid. You got hurt a
lot and you were neglected a lot. Especially
given your early life experiences, is it
understandable to you that you'd be sensitive
to these kinds of reactions and hurt now?

Client: Sure, I guess. But it seems like it hurts too
much.

Therapist: It does hurt a lot. And what I am asking
you is this — does this emotional pain make
sense to you?

Client: Of course it does (she looks sad, but less
distraught).

## New Introjects

In my opinion, one of the single most important things
that can happen in psychotherapy is a change in a client's
internal attitude toward himself/herself. In particular,
there can be a shift away from harshness and criticism
toward an attitude of compassion for the self. In addition
to the interventions mentioned here, which can be helpful,
possibly the most powerful way to facilitate this shift occurs
as an outgrowth of the relationship between the client and
the therapist. The therapist's manner and attitude of
understanding acceptance can, at times, be taken in by our
clients (this may be seen as a form of identification or
introjection). Elements of the therapist's attitude may
include the following:

"Your feelings do matter."

"You can rake yourself over the coals, or you can
choose to be more gentle, decent, and compassionate
toward yourself."

"Your suffering (or sensitivity) is understandable,
especially in the light of certain life experiences."

"You have the right to take your life seriously and to
honor your inner feelings, longings, and needs."

Most of the time, of course, the therapist does not so much speak these words, as convey the message in his or her manner.

Such internal changes for clients sometimes can be realized even in brief therapy, although for those with severe and entrenched self-loathing, longer-term psychotherapy may be necessary. You can often see outward signs of the shift in statements like the following:

- Early in treatment: *"What the hell is wrong with me? I'm just so screwed up!"*

- Later in treatment: *"Of course, I feel this way. I loved her a lot, and I do miss her so much."*

❖ *Cognitions Underlying Feelings of Powerlessness*

The perception of powerlessness or helplessness always intensifies emotional pain. Sometimes this perception is based on hard realities, such as encounters with overwhelming tragedy or trauma. However, very often, the perception is influenced largely by a set of unrealistic, negative cognitions that operate to undermine a person's perception of self-efficacy. Outlined below are the most common of these cognitions, and brief suggested interventions. (For a more comprehensive discussion of cognitive interventions see Beck, 1976, and for cognitive self-help resources see Preston, 1996 and 1997.)

- *Catastrophic Thinking.* The person believes that the worst possible outcome absolutely will happen, which tends to increase the perception of risk and anticipation of helplessness in the wake of imagined catastrophes.

- *Negative Predictions.* This is the tendency to make highly negative, pessimistic predictions about the future, for which there is no evidence. Examples include:
    A single man asks a woman out for a date and is turned down. He thinks, "I'm such a loser. I'm never going to ever find anyone who wants to be with me."

A depressed woman thinks, "I've been depressed for months. I'm never going to get over this. Nothing will ever get me out of this depression."

In both examples, the result is an increased sense of despair and hopelessness.

- *All-or-None Thinking.* This is the tendency to jump to broad, overgeneralized conclusions about oneself or reality. Examples include:

  A woman has just turned in a report at work and her boss criticized the report. She concludes, "I can't do anything right." The reality is that she does many things right; in fact during the past week she has completed five other reports that were well done, but she focuses on the current criticism and arrives at the inaccurate and overgeneralized conclusion, "I can't do anything right."

  A recently divorced man spends a Friday night alone at home. He hoped a friend would call, but none did. He concludes, "No one gives a damn about me." The reality may be that he does in fact have friends and relatives who care a lot about him, but they simply did not call this night.

- *Jumping to Conclusions.* This is the tendency to jump to unwarranted or unrealistic conclusions in the absence of substantial evidence. An example:

  A man applies for a job and is told, "We will call you on Monday if you got the job." By Monday noon he has not heard, and he concludes, "I know I didn't get the job."

  After giving a presentation at work, no one gives a man any direct feedback, thus he concludes, "They all thought my talk was inadequate."

- *Tunnel Vision.* This is the common tendency to focus selectively on negative aspects or shortcomings, to dwell on them and to tune out positive aspects of a situation or oneself. An example:

  A middle-aged man walks by a mirror and notices his pot belly. He thinks, "I'm disgusting. No wonder women aren't interested in me." The fact that he is somewhat overweight may be accurate, but at that moment in front of the mirror this is what he focuses on exclusively. He sees himself as disgusting. It very well may be that he is a kind and sensitive man, attributes that he overlooks as he concludes, "I'm disgusting." He only looks at part of himself, not the whole person.

These various forms of thinking often leave people with firm convictions that:

*"I can't cope well."*

*"All of my efforts are for naught."*

*"Bad outcomes will happen."*

*"I have no personal strengths."*

Each time the person makes such a comment or thinks in this way, it further chips away on his sense of confidence. Perceived self-efficacy erodes, and stress-related symptoms intensify. Cognitive interventions take aim at these processes and attempt to encourage more realistic assessment of current realities, personal resources, and realistic future circumstances.

It must be emphasized that, contrary to some popular misconceptions, cognitive therapy is not the same thing as fostering "positive thinking." It never helps to sugarcoat or distort reality. The aim, rather, is to facilitate accurate reality testing while simultaneously helping the client to face and emotionally experience "necessary pain."

The central features of cognitive interventions are to:
- Be alert to possible cognitive distortions.
- At certain critical moments, choose to intervene.
- Highlight what has been said by the client.
- Encourage the client to explore the facts, assess the situation carefully, and search for the whole truth and nothing but the truth.

Let's illustrate with an example:

Alex: *I am overwhelmed and completely unable to cope with anything!*

Therapist: *Alex, I can see that you are feeling really upset. Let me ask you something, OK?*

Alex: *Sure.*

Therapist: *Clearly you have had some significant troubles dealing with the problem at work. Especially this encounter with your co-worker. I want to ask you to carefully take stock not only of that situation, but of your whole life during the past week. Is it one-hundred percent the case that you have been unable to cope with anything? Give me some specifics.*

Alex: *Well, not one-hundred percent. I think I did a pretty good job handling the situation with my teenage son and I did get the budget report in on time.*

Therapist: *So is this right? You have been able to confront and deal with some pretty tough situations and clearly the situation with the guy at work is very difficult.*

Alex: *Yes.*

The critical elements in this intervention are to resonate with his feelings, and then to challenge him to assess the situation accurately (go from a global to a more specific level of analysis). It is critical to acknowledge his perceptions of trouble at work, but then to help him place this in the context of other realities in which he is coping well. The use of the word *and* is especially important, because it is a way to phrase the statement such that it does not negate his emotional experiences. These kinds of interventions directly aim to improve the accuracy of thinking in a way to combat unrealistic appraisals of powerlessness and helplessness.

Other questions that are often helpful to pose are:

*"Where is the evidence for _____ ?"*

*"Can you be absolutely sure _____ will happen?"*

*"What is the likelihood that _____ will happen?"*

*"Can you look to anything else that is going on in your life that contradicts your conclusions?"*

Cognitive therapists have advocated making such interventions the centerpiece of treatment and also recommend the use of structured within-session and homework cognitive exercises (e.g., three-column technique; see Burns, 1980). At times these techniques can be useful. However, I would like to suggest that occasional cognitive interventions can reasonably be woven into the fabric of all forms of psychotherapy, not necessarily as a preferred general treatment model, but based on the therapist's assessment of a particular need as it arises in a particular moment during a therapy session. Again, I recommend that a technical intervention be based on the assessment of current psychological liabilities and in response to the question, *"What does my client need in this moment?"*

Circumstances where targeted cognitive interventions are especially helpful include:

- Moments of intense affective arousal, where the emotional experience is escalating and the client is feeling out of control

- When you hear strongly voiced conclusions that underscore a client's perception of powerlessness or helplessness

- When the client is making very negative and unwarranted predictions about the future (which generally operate to intensify feelings of powerlessness in the here-and-now)

One of the most common reasons that targeted cognitive interventions fail to alter distorted perceptions or beliefs is that the thinking is being strongly influenced by powerful, underlying schemas. When this is the case, interventions must also be directed toward modification of the schema. We explore this in the next chapter.

# Making an Impact on Negative, Maladaptive Schemas

"No matter what I do, no matter how hard I try, eventually everyone finds out that I am shallow and stupid and without substance. My whole life has been a series of events that always come back to this fundamental truth. I have nothing to offer to anyone, and aside from casual social relationships, I know that I'll never, ever feel loved or cherished by another human being."

*Through the power of our minds, we form concepts that bring order to otherwise random events in ways that allow us to make our way through this life, guided by expectations colored by fear or hope. There is a time for hope and a time for fear. Bringing the same attitude to every situation is not a sign of character, but rather an indication of a character disorder.*

— Sheldon Kopp

Underlying negative schemas profoundly bias perception and cognition. They can affect day-to-day living as people erroneously jump to conclusions, anticipate catastrophes, and make negative predictions. They also largely account for the phenomenon of exquisite emotional vulnerability (the tendency to be especially sensitive to certain specific stressors) and the propensity for engagement in recurrent patterns of maladaptive interpersonal relationships.

Negative schemas are powerful and influential psychological processes that often account for considerable emotional suffering.

Here is where the going gets tough, as we attempt to deal with negative schemas in the context of brief therapy. For some people core schemas are extremely rigid and entrenched, whereas for others, the schemas can be more malleable and open for modification. In clients with significant personality disorders, it is unlikely that shorter-term psychotherapy can afford the opportunity to modify underlying schemas in any significant way. But with higher-level folks we have a better chance of addressing these issues. In this chapter we look at three approaches to modifying maladaptive schemas.

## ❖ *Cognitive Approaches*

The cognitive modification of negative schemas can be approached from two angles. The first is aimed at weakening negative schemas; the second is designed to strengthen positive/adaptive schemas (Elliott and Lassen, 1998). Some authors have suggested providing clients with basic information regarding schema theory, to highlight the role of pervasive early-life experiences and their profound effect on the development of core beliefs (about self, others, and what is anticipated in relationships). This psychoeducational approach can be made more meaningful by offering specific examples from the client's own experiences. Next, it is explained how schemas can often bias perceptions and influence expectations. Again, personally meaningful, concrete examples can help to make this concept understandable and personally relevant. The aim is to help clients appreciate the role of their own unique life experiences, and to "normalize" this human process (rather than pathologize it).

Step two is to work actively with the client to spot here-and-now cognitive distortions, and especially any manifestations of negative self concepts (e.g., comments like "I feel like I am completely worthless," or, "I'm so weak, I can never take a stand for myself"). As is true when challenging cognitive distortions (in the last chapter), it is essential that the therapist first hear and acknowledge such beliefs and the feelings associated with them.

Step three: The crux of the cognitive approach to weakening maladaptive schemas is to work persistently with the client to check the evidence for such beliefs. This is facilitated by following certain guidelines:

- Am I jumping to unwarranted conclusions?
- What is the data?
- Where is the evidence?
- Narrow the focus and look at all the details of a situation.
- Are there any exceptions (information that refutes my conclusions)?
- Would a good friend of mine look at the situation in the same way (this is a good question to ask, to gain perspective) (Elliott and Lassen, 1998).

Conclusions, assumptions, and beliefs are frequently explored during sessions. But for this approach to be truly effective (especially in brief therapy), it is important to encourage the client to practice doing this outside of sessions, in the course of everyday life. Two books written for a lay audience can also be helpful:

- *Why Can't I Get What I Want? Schema Therapy Can Reprogram Your Mental Software and Change Your Life* (Elliott and Lassen, 1998).
- *Reinventing Your Life* (Young and Klosko, 1993).

By a determined and persistent assault on core beliefs (challenging and engaging in more accurate reality testing) one may be able to chip away gradually at negative schemas.

Yet another approach is to use a version of the two-chair technique (popularized by Gestalt therapists). In this intervention the client is encouraged first to occupy one chair, and speak from the part of the self that believes in the negative self-concept capturing the affect. Then switch chairs and have a more realistic and rational self present counterarguments that punch holes in the logic of the negative schema. I have at times suggested that the "rational self" tell the "negative self" some version of the following: "I don't blame you for your beliefs. It is completely understandable that you would come to see things this way, given our early experiences. But you must understand that these beliefs are no longer completely accurate. And these beliefs are not helping us — they are harming us! You need to listen to me now. I am in a better position to see current realities more clearly." When this kind of statement can be spoken (with heart) by the client, it often evokes an emotional response. And in the context of this arousal, such messages often tend to "sink in."

Strengthening adaptive schemas can be encouraged by suggesting that our clients:

- Notice any and all feelings, thoughts, and actions that run contrary to negative self-concepts, and make an effort to attend to this in a deliberate and conscious way (it often helps to keep a list or a diary of "evidence," recording data that refute negative beliefs).

- Make conscious efforts to act in ways that are inconsistent with negative core beliefs (e.g., a man who sees himself as a person without value or worth, may choose to do a "random act of kindness" — be kind or helpful to someone in line at a store or, rather than get irritated with an inconsiderate driver, give extra space on the highway and privately wish the driver well). Such acts need to be things the person genuinely feels OK about doing. Also, afterward, it is important to reflect on what has happened (e.g., "That was a pretty decent thing I just did").

- Be willing to engage in supportive, nurturing "self-talk", e.g. "I can only give my best in each moment"... "I need to give myself a break...be decent to myself...cut myself some slack..." "It's OK to feel compassionate toward myself."
  Again, for these self-statements to be helpful, they must, at least to a degree, be sincerely felt.

None of these approaches can make for quick changes in schemas, but over time they may be able to soften and alter negative beliefs, and provide support for more adaptive and positive views of the self.

---

## EMDR

A new technology has recently been developed by California psychologist Francine Shapiro (1995), called Eye Movement, Desensitization and Reprocessing (EMDR). This set of interventions was initially conceived and developed to help clients suffering from the effects of traumatic stress (see Shapiro's book for a more comprehensive discussion of EMDR). A recent advance in this approach, however, is to use EMDR to modify schemas (i.e., to reprogram or install more realistic and adaptive beliefs and self-talk). The EMDR technique is felt to induce some type of altered state of brain functioning in which desensitization and the acquisition of new cognitions may be facilitated. A more complete description of this approach is beyond the scope of this book, but clinicians should be alert to further developments in this promising technology.

---

### ❖ *Old Wounds and Working Through*

For some clients, very painful or traumatic events dominate their memories. Such material has often been the focus of exploratory psychotherapy, aimed at helping people come to terms with "unfinished business." Beyond some of the more traditional reasons for facing and working through old pain, this can also be an intervention that modifies schemas. I would like to offer an example.

Monica came to therapy suffering from chronic low-grade depression and entrenched feelings of worthlessness. She saw herself largely as a weak and helpless person and a person without a solid, inner sense of self. In relationships she routinely subjugated her own needs and allowed others to dominate her.

In the course of therapy, she began to share her experiences as a young child. Her memories were of countless encounters with a terribly abusive mother. Her mother was a severe alcoholic and a woman prone to frequent episodes of rage directed toward her children. Her father had left the family when she was 6, and throughout the rest of her young life she was subject to her mother's cruelty with no available source of protection or love.

Monica had always remembered those times, but never spoken of them, in large part because she was afraid to open the door to her emotions, fearful that she would be engulfed by overwhelming sadness and fear.

During therapy she was able, for the first time, to share her experiences with her therapist. Sessions were intensely painful, but she felt support by the therapist, and she began to discover inner strengths that she never knew existed.

One very important change that accompanied her process of working through these issues was a modification in an underlying schema. The change can be described as follows:

- *Old schema:* I am a weak, fearful, helpless person. I cannot deal with strong emotions and must run away from them. Also, any suffering I endured as a child was probably deserved. I am worthless and not lovable in the eyes of others.

- *Revised schema:* I have suffered a lot. I also have discovered that I can face tremendous pain and not collapse in the face of it. I do have inner courage. I have learned that I can trust some people with whom I can share personal feelings. Finally, I see my early life from a new perspective; my suffering was not due to deserved punishment for some unknown crime or personal flaws. I was just a kid and I was at the mercy of an emotionally ill, alcoholic mother. I may have been helpless then, but I am now an adult and I have found my strength.

Psychodynamic models have often been criticized for a focus on the past. Current here-and-now beliefs about the self, however, are a legacy of past traumas. One outcome for many people coming to terms with "old wounds" is this kind of significant modification in self-schemas, which certainly has implications for emotional functioning in the present.

*The Impact of the Therapeutic Relationship*

Finally, it is important to note that the modification of inner, negative beliefs can be profoundly influenced by corrective emotional experiences with a genuinely caring therapist. Many people have had numerous encounters with hurtful or destructive people. Plus lots of folks have an uncanny ability either to repeatedly gravitate toward toxic people, or to evoke unpleasant reactions from others. These recurrent experiences often provide powerful ongoing reinforcement for negative schemas. (It's not just early experiences that establish schemas. Ongoing hurtful interactions play a major role in maintaining them.) A therapist's support, care, honesty, and willingness not to judge can be a decisive factor in offering clients a *new experience*. This can contribute to the modification of core schemas. These particular issues are discussed in greater detail in Chapter 20.

# 20 ❖

---

# Repetitive, Maladaptive Interpersonal Patterns

> *There are persons who always find a hair in their plate of soup for the simple reason that, when they sit down before it they shake their heads until one falls in.*
>
> — Christian Friederich Hebbel, *Herodes and Mariamne*

Beyond being innocent victims of fate, many of our clients are unwitting partners in provoking difficult interactions or reengaging in maladaptive patterns of relating with others. It is hard for lay people to fathom this concept. Why in the world, for example, would a person raised in an emotionally abusive environment seek out remarkably similar, toxic relationships in adult life? To understand this phenomenon therapists must be able to appreciate the powerful draw of familiarity. (Even in lower-order species, when young animals are under stress, they seek out attachments with their parents, even when their parent is the source of stress.) A part of this tendency may be etched in our biology. Therapists must also understand how something seemingly quite maladaptive almost always has an underlying adaptational motive (e.g., to feel more secure on familiar turf). And finally, therapists must be keenly alert to the real possibility that we too, will feel the pressure to reenact maladaptive patterns with our patients (they often have powerful, albeit subtle ways of getting others to "dance" with them; we are often coerced into a role of victimizer).

Traditional views of transference focused on perceptual and cognitive distortions that occurred in treatment. The psychotherapy client has often been exposed to powerful experiences early in life, resulting in the gradual development of deeply ingrained schemas (object relations) concerning the self, others, and what is to be anticipated in a relationship. Entering a new relationship (with the therapist) our clients bring with them a lifetime of experiences with others, and are in a state of readiness to anticipate certain things from the stranger/therapist. Such expectations may be realistic, but often they are not. For example, a man accustomed to being ruthlessly criticized and belittled by his parents understandably may be anticipating (consciously or unconsciously) similar treatment from the therapist. Primed to experience this, the client is also quite prone to misread certain cues or to jump to unwarranted conclusions about the therapist, which are in line with preconceived beliefs or worries. Thus, for example, when the therapist meets the person in the waiting room for the first time, and seems a bit aloof, the client may conclude, "He doesn't give a damn about me, he probably thinks I'm a loser." Already there is a perception that may not be at all accurate.

Beyond this internal (cognitive) level, there can also be an interpersonal reenactment. This can occur as the client acts in certain ways to draw from the therapist certain responses that reenact or repeat maladaptive patterns. Let's look at one example to illustrate this point. A very passive and dependent client begins to act in a helpless way, and asks the therapist for advice (this can be seen as the bait). If the therapist takes the bait, responds in kind, and offers advice, then the dance has begun, an interaction where the therapist has been recruited into playing out a scenario starring two characters — a helpless person and a powerful (and infantalizing) doctor. This may momentarily feel good for the client (it's familiar), but it may ultimately contribute to keeping him/her operating in an infantile way. The theme of the interaction is, "I am weak. I can't help myself. Thus I need to turn to others to fix me, to advise me, to tell me what to do." In addition to transferential cognitive distortions, if the client can actually provoke the therapist into some sort of hurtful interaction, then a maladaptive interaction has, in fact, recurred.

Such an interpersonal behavior (e.g., expression of helplessness and passivity) is likely to permeate most of the client's other relationships in life. If the therapist joins in with the dance, it can only serve to keep the client stuck. If this occurs, the therapist's attitude and treatment of the client can also verify long-held self-schemas: "I am incapable of growing up and meeting life's challenges. Even this therapist can see that, and that's why he/she is giving me advice." Thus we have what amounts to self-propagating vicious circles, which are likely to be constantly played out in numerous, contemporary relationships.

To be more helpful in promoting change and growth, the therapist needs to be alert to these "invitations to dance," and respond in ways that do not perpetuate the problem, but change it. This requires first and foremost that we are alert to these issues as they begin to emerge (which is often difficult to do, since many aspects of our experiences with our clients may involve very subtle pressures and pulls to react in these familiar, albeit maladaptive ways). All therapists from time to time take the bait before we know what is happening. So, it's important to see it coming, and it's also important to know what to do once you've been recruited into the reciprocal role.

### ❖ Spotting the Bait

One of the most useful ways to identify and understand what may be occurring in the therapeutic interaction is periodically to stop and consider three sources of data, by asking the following questions: What are the dominant interactional themes reported by my client in (1) significant early relationships (e.g. with parents) and (2) important relationships during adult life? (3) What is occurring in the therapeutic interaction (including client behaviors and any countertransference issues)?

Let's consider two examples:

*Mr. A.:* 1. Always remembers feeling criticized by his father. "In his eyes, I could never do anything right."

2. With his wife and several of his supervisors at work, Mr. A. reports frequently feeling criticized and being treated as if he is inept.

3. In therapy sessions, Mr. A. will often make

comments such as, "I just don't know what to do. Do you think I did the right thing?" (i.e. sets self up by inviting a judgmental remark from the therapist). Also, the therapist, in a way uncharacteristic for him, has found himself feeling critical toward Mr. A. or actually telling Mr. A. what he should do.

*Mr. B.:*  1. Recalls, painfully, his father and mother mocking him for being a helpless "crybaby."

2. Often emotionally collapses at times of marital conflict. In the aftermath of this, his wife often gives in and concedes to his position.

3. In therapy sessions, Mr. B. often has a hard time ending on time. And his therapist has noticed that she has let sessions run over past the appropriate stopping time. She is generally quite good about maintaining such limits, but is experiencing more difficulties with Mr. B.

With these sources of data we are able to triangulate; the information from these three vantage points can often, in a remarkable way, clarify what is happening in the therapeutic relationship. In particular, it is helpful to be especially alert to any countertransference reactions (i.e., those emotional responses or interactions on the part of the therapist that are either intense and/or uncharacteristic for the therapist). These often signal that we have taken the bait and are a part of a reenactment.

Repetitive, maladaptive interactions with others are such a common source of emotional distress that once identified, they can become the target for therapeutic interventions. Let's now take a look at strategies that can address this particular set of psychological liabilities.

## ❖ Interventions

Two general strategies may be helpful when the decision has been made to try to alter repetitive maladaptive interactions. The first involves a concept originally articulated by Franz Alexander (Alexander & French, 1946), the *corrective emotional experience*. This concept is frequently misunderstood to mean simply providing a benign, supportive interaction for the client. Alexander appreciated that clients often "pull" for certain responses from others (baiting the trap), and that almost always this is not done in a conscious, willful way. Generally, it emerges in a very automatic and unconscious manner. Providing a corrective emotional experience means being able to understand and appreciate the true nature of particular recurrent patterns of interaction, and then to resist the urge to join in the dance. When the therapist can successfully refuse to repeat, there is an opportunity for a new experience for the client (remarkably, such new experiences may be singular in the client's life). Not repeating maladaptive patterns of interaction tends to be an intervention in itself.

It is important to note that when this refusal to join in the maladaptive dance is first experienced by the client, it can result in some distress. We must keep in mind that many clients have become accustomed to experiencing the same general response from almost everyone (e.g., others being disgusted, disinterested, critical, judging, hostile, infantalizing, rejecting). Not to experience the anticipated, familiar interactions can be destabilizing, and may initially provoke anxiety. It may also motivate new efforts on the part of the client (unconsciously) designed to provoke the anticipated hurtful interaction. But, if the therapist can persevere and resist the strong pull to repeat, over time this new experience can operate in two ways to help our client.

First, it can offer a new experience that may be healing in itself (possibly, for the first time, to feel that another person is genuinely concerned or interested in understanding, rather than sitting in judgment). This can, in a powerful way, help to modify underlying negative schemas. Second, if the therapist can repeatedly demonstrate that he or she will not treat the client in hurtful ways, at some point the client will begin to experience a deep sense of safety. "Where I have always been hurt, judged, ignored in the past, it really is not happening here." The repeated experience of being treated in this fashion (respected, believed, cared about) can help the client to open inner doors. It is only in this atmosphere of safety that many clients can feel secure enough to risk increased vulnerability.

## ❖ Passing the Test

An interesting perspective has been offered by the Mt. Zion Psychotherapy group (Weiss, 1971). They have proposed a theory referred to as the Control-Mastery model. Central to this model is the belief that all clients must feel safe, and openness or vulnerability cannot occur in psychotherapy until the client is assured of the degree of safety provided by the therapist. Safety is determined by the use of a *test*. The test can be seen as a type of interpersonal maneuver. It is not done consciously, but rather is an automatic and habitual style of interaction that is initiated in all interpersonal relationships. The client says or does something and the other person's response helps the client assess, "Is this relationship safe?" Two issues are being addressed with the "test": (1) Will this person (the therapist) repeat hurtful patterns of interaction that I have become accustomed to experiencing? (2) Will this be a safe place to risk revealing myself (allowing vulnerability and sharing inner secrets)?

When the therapist does not take the bait, and does not participate in the "dance," he or she has passed the test, and a greater degree of safety is forged in the relationship.

Let's take a look at six of the most common sets of tests.

1. *Will you criticize me?* (shame me, scorn me?)
   A bitter and irritable woman tells her therapist about a number of times in which she was quite nasty and degrading to others. Her therapist personally finds her profoundly degrading behavior toward others to be disgusting, although he is able to resist acting out these feelings, and maintains a neutral posture. This is the essence of the test, and the therapist passes numerous tests with this woman. Four months into treatment (presumably after sensing that she would really not be criticized or rejected by the therapist) she begins to open up about terrible abuse she experienced as a young child.

2. *Will you attack me?* (or get angry with me?)

A very distraught borderline woman comes to her first session. Her initial comment is, "You God-damned doctors don't know what you are doing! You don't know how to help anyone!" The therapist feels assaulted, but is able to reply calmly, "It sounds like you really want to be helped." The woman settles down. As therapy progresses, it will come as no surprise to learn that this woman has seen nine previous therapists, has gotten in fights with each of them, and abruptly stormed out of each therapy in an uproar. Also no surprise, her father was explosive, unpredictable, harsh, and physically abusive. Inside of this caustic woman is a wounded, frightened child, which does not become apparent for a long time, as the therapist is subjected to and ultimately passes numerous "tests."

3. *Will you infantilize me?*

A physician enters treatment stating, "I just need some advice on how to make decisions about my career." He is full of self-doubts and reported problems with decision-making in general. "What do you think I should do?" is a common question heard during therapy sessions. His history reveals that his father always told him he was immature and that he made bad decisions. He rarely feels supported in any independent actions that he takes. Currently he is often berated by his wife, who accuses him of being "weak" and childish. Notice that from his opening statement, he is inviting the therapist to "tell me what I should do." This plea is punctuated by his rather helpless and pathetic demeanor. To take this bait would keep him stuck. The therapist has to endure many challenging moments as the man almost begs to be told what to do. Only by resisting the pull and passing many difficult tests is the therapist able to maintain a stance which supports the doctor's own autonomy.

4. *Will you join me in defending, glossing over, or minimizing my pain?*

This test can often be spotted by comments such as:

*"Oh, I'm OK...it's no big deal."*

*"I'll get over this eventually."*

*"It never helps to cry."*

In each instance, the client may seem to be looking at the therapist for verification. If the therapist even subtly agrees, then the dance has begun. A way to pass these kinds of tests is to recognize them as resistances, not to collude, and to say something that acknowledges the underlying emotional pain.

5. *Will you rescue me?*
   The plea here is to have the therapist rescue the client from experiencing painful feelings. This can be powerful, in moments when the client begins to feel strong emotions. Often a look of desperation or helplessness provokes a rescue response from the therapist, who rushes in to change the subject, or otherwise divert the focus away from pain. Clearly, there are appropriate times for intervening to reduce emotional arousal. The rescue test I am addressing here pertains to clients who have adequate ego strength but doubt their ability to face, head-on, intense emotions.

   Often they have been treated by others as being weak or emotionally fragile. They have not had others to believe in their abilities to find inner strength and rise to the occasion. To pass this test is often also a way of giving our vote of confidence in their inner abilities to cope during difficult times.

6. *Can I trust you?*
   Clients often do not want, but certainly need, consistency and firmness offered by maintaining the therapeutic frame. This is done in a number of ways, such as starting and stopping sessions on time, dealing with issues within the session rather than between sessions (except in the case of true emergencies), maintaining strictly professional boundaries, and so on. Many clients (especially

those with more severe personality disorders) test their therapists by trying to bend or violate boundaries. (Many of these people grew up in boundary-less homes.) Failing these tests will show the client that she cannot fully count on the therapist to be firm, and this can cause the client to become more and more destabilized. Conversely, although many such clients don't especially like the rules and limits of therapy, when such issues of frame are maintained, ultimately it can be helpful. The therapist can eventually be trusted. The predictability and consistency can operate like an anchor and contribute significantly to the client's experience of safety.

Interventions that address the problem of repetitive, maladaptive interactions center around the therapist's ability to spot and understand what is occurring in the moment between therapist and client. Next it is important to resist steadfastly the often-powerful pull to repeat. This alone can help break up the repetitive pattern, and can contribute to other changes in therapy by furthering the creation of a safe environment.

One additional intervention strategy can also be helpful.

### ❖ *Developing a Narrative*

Strupp and Binder (1984) offer another approach that can help break up repetitive interpersonal patterns. Central to this approach is the notion we have discussed in which people play out roles and scripts, and recruit others into "dancing with them" in ways that are largely unconscious. What may seem obvious to an observer may be completely unknown to the client (i.e., his/her tendency to reengage in certain maladaptive relationships). This approach involves developing a narrative.

The key elements to constructing a narrative include ascertaining the following:

1. *Phase one:* Preexisting, self-defeating expectations (what is anticipated in new relationships, e.g., "ultimately the other will see me as boring and stupid, and will want nothing to do with me").

2. *Phase two:* Maladaptive interactions/behaviors (e.g., being primed to experience rejection, the person does not seek out social interaction with others, does not make eye contact, does not say "good morning").

3. *Phase three:* Interactions result in negative self-appraisals (e.g., people respond to the person's aloofness by avoiding him and thus he often concludes, "See, they aren't friendly toward me, they probably think I am boring and stupid"). This results in ongoing experiences that constantly validate and perpetuate negative self-beliefs.

Once the therapist has heard the description of several such experiences, and questions the client regarding expectations and after-the-fact self-appraisals, a tentative description may be shared with the client. It can begin with a statement such as this, "I've been thinking about some of the situations that you have described and I have a hunch about what's happening. I'd like to share this with you, and please tell me what you think." Then the therapist can briefly sketch out a narrative that, in a sense, tells a story connecting expectations, client behaviors, responses from others, and after-the-fact self-appraisals.

For this intervention to be helpful three ingredients are necessary:

1. There must be an established therapeutic alliance, primarily so the client does not feel criticized.

2. It must be based on fairly solid data, and thus should not be formulated until the therapist has heard at least a couple of descriptions of interactions, and sees a recurrent theme emerge.

3. It should be offered in a tentative manner.

The goals of the intervention are to bring into clearer awareness the role of preexisting expectations and how these beliefs and feelings may influence both here-and-now perceptions (or distortions) and resulting client behavior. Also, the hope is to demonstrate how the client's own behavior may be playing a critical role in provoking others to respond. Finally, you are pointing out that it is very natural to arrive at negative self-appraisals, but such conclusions may be based on faulty thinking. For example, "They don't speak to me because I'm boring," might be more accurately stated, "Maybe they don't speak to me because I'm not looking at them or being friendly."

If the formulation is accurate, if it can be taken in and shared by the client, and if the client senses that the therapist is trying to understand and to help (rather than be critical) the intervention may be effective. In part, this approach, by bringing certain behavioral sequences into awareness, breaks up the habitual, automatic quality of the patterns. Clients are more likely to be aware of internal cognitions the next time they confront certain social situations. This approach is most potent when it is successfully combined with appropriate corrective experiences and the passing of tests, as described earlier.

# Underdeveloped Sense of Self

"Most of the time, I know how I feel, I know what I want, I have my own opinions, I know what matters to me. But every time I get in an emotional argument with my husband, I go into a tail-spin. For days I doubt myself. I question if my reactions were legitimate. I just completely lose confidence in myself."

An important area of psychological functioning is the experience of an internal sense of "self." This construct is somewhat elusive and hard to define, but it is a very important aspect of one's psychological life. It is rare that clients come into therapy exclaiming that "my *self* is underdeveloped." However, if we listen carefully to our clients, numerous outward signs of an impaired self can be identified. The 11 areas listed in Figure 21-A outline the manifestations of the client's self.

Although signs of an underdeveloped self are seen most often in people with severe personality disorders, these issues are evident across a broad array of levels of functioning.

A number of interventions can help to foster the development of a more solid self:

- Maintaining clear boundaries (e.g., keeping the relationship strictly professional; starting and stopping sessions on time).

- Treating all clients as if they are responsible adults (even if they are emotionally immature). For example, this can take place as the therapist expects clients to pay their fee, as agreed, to attend sessions, to observe certain limits, and so on.

*Figure 21-A*                                            *Manifestations of the SELF*

| Well-Developed SELF | Underdeveloped SELF |
|---|---|
| 1. Aware of inner beliefs, needs, values, feelings. | 1. Unaware of inner needs, etc. or only vaguely perceived. |
| 2. Feels a sense of "ownership" of inner needs, feelings, etc. Often experienced as understandable and legitimate (even when unpleasant). | 2. Experiences feelings or needs as "happening *to* me" (not from within myself); needs may be perceived as ego alien; may be disowned. |
| 3. Can retain values, beliefs, feelings, and needs even when in the presence of powerful others. | 3. Likely to abandon inner beliefs, needs, etc., quickly compromising to placate others. (This may or may not be experienced consciously or as a choice.) |
| 4. Can make clear, unambiguous statements of inner feelings, beliefs, needs, etc. | 4. Cloaks expressions of inner feelings in hesitancy, apologies, or minimization. |
| 5.  Has a constant inner sense of "I" or "SELF" across a broad array of situations/circumstances. | 5. Has an ill-defined sense of inner self or constantly shifting, fragmented sense of self. The person is often confused about how he or she really feels or what he or she really wants. |
| 6. Pursues personally meaningful goals; life is lived in accord with inner desires and values. | 6. Occupational and other major life pursuits are ill-defined, chaotic, or undirected. There is a lack of clarity regarding major life goals and decisions. |
| 7. Has an inner sense of "centeredness" analogous to an anchor or ballast in a ship that provides an experience of stability, especially during stressful times. | 7. Has an internal sense of chaos, fragmentation, and instability. |
| 8. Has clear self-other boundaries. Able to be empathic yet also maintain separateness. | 8. Has very permeable boundaries. An example is when another person is sad, the client resonates with the other, become sad as well. |
| 9. Able to internally self-generate feelings of worth. | 9. Relies inordinately on others to provide reassurance. |
| 10. Can take an assertive stand on things that matter. | 10. Demonstrates passivity or subjugation. Quickly abandons own beliefs, needs, etc. |
| 11. Trusts hunches and intuitive feelings. | 11. Unaware of or discounts hunches and intuitions. |

- Showing our clients that we respect their emerging autonomy, e.g.:

  *"I want to know what you think."*
  *"What is your opinion?"*

  *"Regardless of what Gail thought, how did you see the situation?"*

- Underscoring comments that appear to be expressions of our client's true inner self:

  *"It sounds like that matters a lot to you."*

  *"It seems to me that you were really able to take a stand, and speak out about what is most important to you."*

  *"If I'm hearing you right, it seems that this meant a lot to you."*

- Any approach that encourages or reinforces self-expression. One of the most powerful experiences is when people are able to reveal highly personal feelings or experience vulnerability, and have a corrective experience (i.e., to feel genuinely understood and accepted by the therapist, rather than experiencing shame).

- Flagging and acknowledging spontaneous comments that appear to be expressions of the self, for example, a female client says, "He and I absolutely did not agree on how to handle this situation." (This statement reveals (1) an awareness of her own beliefs and point of view and (2) a defined boundary between herself and the other person.) Therapist: "It seems obvious that the two of you did not see eye-to-eye."

  Client: *I just had this gut feeling that he didn't really give a damn about me.*
  Therapist: *So you trusted your intuition.*

> Client:  *I feel I had a right to be upset about it —*
> *she was being very degrading.*
> Therapist:  *You felt that your reaction was legitimate?*
> Client:  *Yes!*

> Client:  *No matter what she said, I felt I did a lot to*
> *help out and I feel proud of myself.*

This kind of spontaneous statement can also be a good barometer of improvement that can be tracked across sessions.

- Encouraging the client to be assertive in life outside of therapy sessions, i.e., to speak out, to take a stand, or to interact more directly with others (this takes inner feelings, needs, and so on from the intrapsychic to the interpersonal arena).

- Fostering the development of life-style habits that provide health and comfort for the client (e.g., "care and feeding of the self" — adequate rest, good nutrition, exercise, fresh air, recreation, humor, relaxation, a balance in work and play, establishing realistic expectations for oneself, and occasional splurges).

- Encourage the use of "*self*-supporting homework," such as making a list of "what matters most to me in my life" and posting it on the bathroom mirror. Each day writing down on paper two things: "Things that I did today that were expressions of my true self," and a brief "gratitude list" (i.e. listing several things for which you feel grateful on this particular day). This can help the client to acknowledge and keep in clearer awareness the things that matter most.

- If so inclined, help clients identify meaningful activities or "causes," and get involved.

- Helping the client to develop an attitude of compassion for himself/herself.

In addition to simply feeling good, when people experience an increased sense of self they often also report the following: more emotional sturdiness, feelings (even painful ones) seem more "real" and more understandable, and there is a greater general sense of aliveness.

Often a degree of enhanced sense of self can be realized in brief therapy. However, what is more commonly seen is the beginning of movement in this direction, which is likely to continue after treatment ends. Ultimately the growth of the self is not a finite end state, but an ongoing experience in living.

# 22

# *Emotional Dyscontrol*

"I tell myself that it's not that big a deal, everyone goes through difficult times. But since getting fired from my job I have times when I think that I am about to completely lose my mind. I get so incredibly overwhelmed, like my head starts spinning, I shake all over, I feel frantic, I think I'm going to explode or that I'll just start crying and screaming and won't be able to stop!"

Overwhelming emotional states are a common experience in many psychiatric disorders. They may be part of recurring neuropsychiatric illnesses such as bipolar disorder, or a defining characteristic of certain personality disorders (e.g., histrionic or borderline personality disorder). And states of intense emotion are certainly common in acute disorders such as reactive depressions or post-traumatic stress disorders. Each disorder requires specific and possibly unique interventions. In this chapter, however, we look at several strategies that may be appropriate for targeting emotional dyscontrol in general.

## ❖ Non Nocere Primum: Do No Harm

> *Avoid techniques of desperation. Heroism is the shortest career there is and often fatal.*
> — Harry Wilmer, *Practical Jung*

First and foremost, it is important to appreciate that in true *dyscontrol*, intense affect is so powerful and disruptive that people find it hard or impossible to process the experience.

227

Thus interventions that avoid throwing gas on the fire and aim for better defensive control and stabilization are required. For this reason, a host of common therapeutic approaches should be avoided (i.e., interventions that are evocative or those that tamper with resistances).

### Neurobiological Stabilization: The Role of Psychotropic Medications

❖

Intense emotional experiences are often amplified because of underlying neurobiological factors (e.g., dysregulation of certain neurotransmitter systems in the brain, or the impact of significant sleep deprivation). In the next chapter we talk in detail about approaches designed to reduce emotional vulnerability associated with brain dysfunction. Here I would like to address, briefly, the use of psychopharmacology.

Psychiatric medications are being used more and more as an adjunct to brief psychotherapy, for three reasons: (1) Many of the newer medications have better side-effect profiles and are safer (less toxic), for example, the SSRI's (serotonergic antidepressants — Prozac, Paxil, Serzone, and Zoloft); (2) Such medications have been found to be effective in treating not only major depression, but a host of psychiatric conditions (e.g., panic disorder, OCD, PTSD, borderline personality disorder); (3) With appropriate use, and in combination with brief psychotherapy, we are now able to help more people within the confines of short-term treatment. One of the more common effects of SSRI medication is enhanced emotional control. This appears to be due to the role of serotonin as an important inhibitory neurotransmitter in key limbic areas of the brain.

It should also be noted that benzodiazepines (antianxiety/minor tranquilizers such as Xanax, Librium, Ativan, Valium, and so on) are prescribed for a number of people experiencing significant emotional dyscontrol. With many individuals, the short-term use of these medications can be both safe and effective. However, there are two notable groups in which treatment with benzodiazepines is risky: (1) borderline personality disorder (studies indicate that the use of benzodiazepines can actually result in disinhibition and thus exacerbate emotional outbursts and suicidal impulses), and (2) In individuals with a history of substance abuse/alcoholism (in this group, benzodiazepines can clearly become drugs of abuse).

A more comprehensive discussion of psychopharm-acology is beyond the scope of this book. The interested reader is referred to Preston et al. (1997) for a more thorough discussion of psychiatric medication treatment.

## ❖ *Cognitive Interventions*

It is human nature during times of significant emotional arousal to experience three cognitive phenomena that tend to greatly amplify affective intensity. The first of these is catastrophic thinking. The core element in such thinking is the conclusion that the absolutely worst possible outcome will happen. In the emotion of the moment, critical thinking can become suspended. At times of intense dyscontrol, the therapist can actively interrupt the avalanche of catastrophic thoughts and encourage more careful thinking and reality testing. Let's consider an example:

Debra: *Oh God* (sobbing and trembling), *I am falling apart. I know I'm going to lose it, and then I'll lose my job, and they'll take my kids away.*

Therapist: *Debra, I want to interrupt* (the therapist speaks in a firm but compassionate voice). *It's important that I say something to you. It's clear that this has been very upsetting for you.* (Note: It is critical to validate her experience of intense, painful emotions.) *Let's stop and consider the situation very carefully. I want to think this situation through with you, and let's slow down and take a close look at what is happening* (the therapist is stating the intent of the intervention: "Stop and think").

The therapist can then ask Debra to engage in more systematic thinking in trying to get clear about exactly what has happened ("just the facts, ma'am"), and to be watchful for any arbitrary conclusions or other cognitive distortions. If these are noted, it is important to help her challenge them. Have her carefully consider the "evidence," especially as this relates to any negative predictions. Encourage her to pay particular attention to the distinction between "the negative outcome absolutely will occur" versus "it may occur" (changing high probability to an assessment of likelihood or possibility). Help her to recall past times when she encountered similar events or experienced intense feelings and ask her to reflect on the outcome — how long did the upset last; how did she cope with it? A second common class of cognitions that can powerfully intensify emotions is what has become known as "should statements."

*"It shouldn't happen!"*

*"I should have known better!"*

*"I shouldn't be so sensitive!"*

*"He shouldn't treat me that way!"*

Add to the list words such as "must, have to, and ought to." Thinking with shoulds creates a perception of the person as a victim. It is a cognition that accentuates helplessness and powerlessness. Interventions can focus on such statements. The intention is not to deny or minimize real feelings, but rather to rephrase/reconceptualize from a different vantage point, which often rather quickly turns down the volume on strong emotions. Examples of alternatives to the previous statements are:

*"It's not a matter of should or shouldn't. The truth is that it has happened, and I don't like it one bit!"*

*"I wish I had known better, but I didn't, and it's not a crime or a sin; it's just unfortunate."*

*"I do have strong feelings about this."*

*"It's not whether he should or shouldn't treat me this way. The bottom line is that I don't like the way he has acted toward me!"*

When clients are encouraged to adopt this perspective they generally feel less helpless and more empowered; it also often reduces emotional intensity while continuing to acknowledge and honor true feelings.

One of the most effective affect modulation strategies is the use of language and critical thinking. As clients are encouraged to talk out loud about inner experiences, and challenged to think accurately, the therapist can often facilitate a rapid reduction in affective intensity.

A third very common experience in the midst of an affective storm is the loss of perspective. One of the more helpful interventions that aims to help the client reestablish a realistic perspective is what I call the 60-second *reality check*. This can be done at the therapist's direction in the session. Also, a copy of Figure 22-A can be given to the client to use at times of emotional upheaval.

---

*Figure 22-A*                    *60-Second Reality Check*

During times of stress, it's quite common to experience moments of very strong, upsetting feelings. But just a minute can help you regain perspective and reduce distress.

As soon as something triggers a very strong feeling of irritation, sadness, fear, or anger, take 60 seconds to go through the following list:

- *Does what just happened really matter to me?*
- *In the grand scheme of things, how big a deal is it? Is it likely to seem like a catastrophe in 24 hours? A week?*
- *Am I taking this too personally?*
- *If I react now, will it probably help or make matters worse?*
- *Would it make sense to take time to think through the situation, then decide how to react?*
- *Are my thoughts/actions helping me or hurting me right now? Is what I'm telling myself about the situation accurate or might I be jumping to conclusions?*

As you answer the questions, don't try to talk yourself out of feeling the way you do. Instead, reflect on how you really see the situation. By avoiding an impulsive, stress-induced reaction, you can choose a wise response.

---

## ❖ The Therapeutic Relationship

In the course of daily living, when most people become quite emotional, three responses from others are typically encountered: (1) Others become overwhelmed or frightened and pull away; (2) Others also become upset, which can exacerbate the crisis; or (3) Others offer consoling comments, "There, there; it can't be all that bad," often leaving the upset party feeling dismissed and unheard.

Clearly one of the most important stabilizing features in psychotherapy is the therapist's ability to be present and yet not to be blown away by the force of intense emotions. The key to accomplishing this is the therapist's ability (1) to act as an emotional "shock absorber" (endure the intensity); (2) to remain steady and not overreact; (3) to maintain perspective; (4) to show compassion; (5) to take action and intervene (as mentioned above) so that things are not allowed to escalate too much; and (6) to be watchful for possible, nonhelpful countertransference reactions (especially common if the emotions are directed toward the therapist). As therapists, we all know, that this is often a tall order; this is where our training and our own personal psychotherapy are indispensable.

# 23

# *Neurobiological Vulnerability*

As mentioned in the previous chapter, many, if not most, psychiatric disorders may involve some degree of disruption in neurobiological integrity. This may be due either to the disorder involving a primary dysregulation of neurotransmitters, or the biological effects of stress, especially those attributed to sleep disturbances. Pharmacological approaches can be appropriate interventions with a number of clients. In this chapter we will look at nonmedical strategies, which can probably be recommended to almost all clients seen in brief psychotherapy.

## Stabilizing Sleep Cycles

> *Sleep that knits up the raveled sleeve of care*
> *the death of each day's life, sore labor's*
> *bath, balm of hurt minds, great nature's*
> *second course, chief nourisher in life's feast.*
> — William Shakespeare, *Macbeth*

Sleep is a very fragile biological function; in many people it is easily interrupted by even minor stresses. Significant sleep disturbances can have a profound effect on cognitive and emotional functions. During times of crisis, almost without exception, most people experience at least some degree of sleep impairment.

### Sleep Disturbances

Studies have found that all people go through the various stages of sleep each night. These stages range from light sleep to deep sleep and are measured precisely with an electroencephalograph (EEG), which measures brain activity. Sleep is roughly divided into two types: (1) REM (rapid eye movement) sleep; and (2) non-REM sleep. During REM sleep, the brain is highly active. This is the time during which most dreaming occurs. Non-REM sleep contains four stages ranging from 1 to 4, with stages 3 and 4 containing a particular type of brain wave activity referred to as delta sleep (or deep sleep). Most stage 3 and stage 4 sleep is seen during the first half of the night. REM periods become longer as the night progresses (see Figure 23-A).

Experimental studies have shown dramatically that if the amount of deep sleep is reduced or eliminated, there are significant consequences for the individual. In particular, often after only two nights of sleep deprivation (selectively deprived of stages 3 and 4), volunteer subjects experience the following:

- Significant daytime fatigue

- Difficulties with thinking (e.g., poor concentration, impaired memory, and so on)

- Changes in emotional functioning, including: irritability, lowered frustration tolerance, and decreased ability to control or inhibit the expression of emotions in general.

Increased anxiety often has an impact on sleep. It can result in insomnia (especially *initial insomnia,* difficulty falling asleep) and, in general, an erosion of deep sleep. In addition, a number of substances can interfere with sleep, the most common of which are alcohol and caffeine.

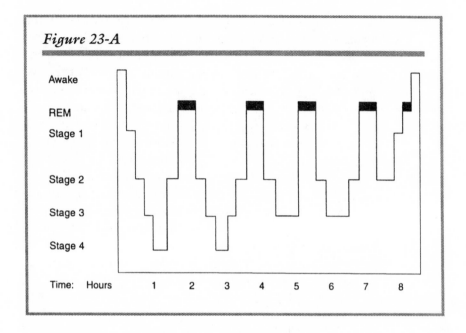

### Figure 23-A

## Alcohol Use

Alcohol, if ingested in moderate to heavy amounts, causes sedation and may help people to fall asleep. Many people when under stress turn to alcohol to numb emotional pain and to fall asleep. Unfortunately, alcohol is a solution that backfires. A few hours after ingesting alcohol, some of the metabolic by-products of alcohol hit the brain and actually cause arousal. Many people who abuse alcohol will report such middle-of-the-night awakenings.

## Caffeine Use

It is widely known that caffeine can interfere with sleep; it is especially notorious for causing initial insomnia. For this reason, many people avoid the use of caffeine in the afternoon or evening. However, caffeine use can also cause an increase in middle-of-the-night awakenings and a decrease in the total amount of deep sleep (*DSM-IV*, APA, 1994). It is important to emphasize that this can occur even in the absence of initial insomnia. So many of our clients who use a lot of caffeine do not experience initial insomnia, and thus conclude that the caffeine does not affect their sleep (unaware that, although they may be sleeping, it is an inefficient kind of sleep; lacking the very important stages of *deep* sleep). If you talk to clients about reducing caffeine, many will pooh-pooh the idea, not appreciating how much their caffeine intake is actually causing sleep impairment and the resulting increase in emotional dyscontrol.

It is important to take a caffeine history on all patients. It takes two minutes and is a high-yield intervention. The general guidelines are that if the person ingests more than 250 mg. of caffeine per day (regardless of the time of day) the caffeine is likely to affect sleep. An amount of 500 mg. or more per day is *highly* likely to cause a sleep disturbance. A list of caffeine-containing products is provided in Figure 23-B.

It is amazing how so many clients get into the habit of drinking a lot of caffeine, especially when they are under stress. Caffeine combats fatigue and provides some transient mood elevation. However, in the long run, it further compromises the person's abilities for maintaining emotional stability. Encouraging clients to eliminate caffeine often makes a big difference (but anticipate some resistance from them when you suggest this, because most simply will not believe that it can really help). The key to reducing caffeine use is to have the client cut back gradually, over a period of three to four weeks. Abrupt discontinuation can result in caffeine withdrawal symptoms (jitteriness, anxiety, insomnia, and headaches).

### Figure 23-B                    *Caffeine Content of Common Substances*

| Beverages | | | Over-the-Counter Drugs | |
|---|---|---|---|---|
| Coffee | 6 oz | 150 mg | Appetite-control pills | 100-200 mg |
| Decaf coffee | 6 oz | 5 mg | NoDoz | 100 mg |
| Tea | 6 oz | 50 mg | Vivarin | 200 mg |
| Hot cocoa | 6 oz | 15 mg | Anacin | 32 mg |
| Caffeinated | | | Exedrin | 65 mg |
| Soft drinks | 12 oz | 40-60 mg | Midol | 132 mg |
| | | | Vanquish | 33 mg |
| **Prescription Drugs** | | | Triaminicin | 30 mg |
| Cafergot | | 100 mg | Dristan   16 mg | |
| Fiorinal | | 140 mg | | |
| Darvon compound | | 32 mg | Chocolate candy bar | 15-40 mg |

Source: FDA National Center: Drugs and Biologics (as cited in Avis, 1993).

## Circadian Cycles

The stabilization of the circadian (24-hour cycles) rhythm can also aid in restoring normal sleep. Three actions have been shown to be quite helpful in bringing this about.

1. Establish regular bedtimes and times for awakening. This may not be agreeable to many clients, but it is often very successful if done correctly. The circadian rhythm organizes itself around highly regular patterns of exposure to light and dark, and this is best achieved by maintaining a regular sleeping schedule.

2. A second activity also helps stabilize the circadian rhythm: exposure to early morning bright light. This is best done for at least one hour upon awakening and with exposure to very bright light (2500 lux or above); this can be accomplished by exposure to outside light or the use of a commercially available light box.

3. The third activity is regular exercise. A program of regular exercise (especially aerobic-level exercise) has many benefits (e.g., improved physical health, increases in brain serotonin levels, enhanced physical pain tolerance, etc.). Exercise has also been shown to increase the amount of time spent in deep sleep.

Simply suggesting to clients that they reduce alcohol and caffeine, get bright light exposure, and exercise is often unsuccessful. They won't take the suggestion seriously or they will have difficulty following through. I have found it significantly more helpful to give them a brief lecture about sleep cycles, point out the need for deep sleep and how this has an impact on emotional functioning, and then introduce the issues involving caffeine, exercise, and so on. It is often helpful to tell them that taking action to change these habits is a very direct way to regain at least some control over their brain functioning and, ultimately, their ability for increased emotional self-control. Making such changes empowers them. These are direct, concrete actions that allow us to get more out of brief therapy.

---

This chapter is adapted from Preston (1997) with permission: New Harbinger Publications, Oakland.

# The Keys to
# Keeping Treatment Brief

In this final chapter I would like to highlight six key factors that are important in time-limited treatment. These factors have received general support from most clinicians who have written about brief therapy.

## ❖ Rapid Assessment

As addressed in early chapters, in brief therapy we must hit the ground running. Central to this is the need to arrive at preliminary diagnostic impressions — hopefully by the end of the first session. This will guide the therapist in the establishment of fairly specific treatment goals, the determination of realistic, desired outcomes, and initial ideas about the class of interventions that are most likely to facilitate change. As noted earlier, two primary assessment questions are, "Why isn't life working for this individual client at this particular time in his/her life?" and, "Is this person a good brief therapy candidate?"

## ❖ Deciding Upon a Focus

Most clinicians writing about brief therapy agree that it is essential (usually toward the end of the first session) to encourage the client to define a single focus for the therapy. Many of our clients may have a multitude of problems, and to try and address them all in brief therapy is not realistic. Thus, a therapist might say,

> *"Today we've talked about several important issues in your life that are a concern. Given that you are*

*beginning brief therapy, and our time is precious
(limited), I would like to encourage you to think
carefully and to decide which one of these areas
stands out as most important to you at this time in
your life. Obviously, all of these concerns are
important to you, but I think it is essential that the
two of us mutually agree on one main problem or
issue and then be committed to having this be the
primary focus of our therapy. Given the time we
have to work together, it will be necessary to keep
focused on that one main area of concern."*

For many therapists this seems rather directive (and it
is; the therapist is structuring and limiting the focus of the
treatment from the outset). However, if this is not done
early on, then the prospects for a successful outcome in
brief therapy will be significantly reduced. Short-term
psychotherapy is not a place to fix all life's problems, but it
can often provide an opportunity to hone in and focus on
a particular issue. If a single focus can be delineated and
agreed on, and if the therapist can gently but firmly keep
each session directed toward the identified topic, the odds
of success are greatly enhanced.

### ❖ Setting Time Limits

It is generally very helpful to be clear from the start
regarding the number of sessions you are planning to offer.
This provides a frame or structure that often can make
things happen. With long-term or open-ended treatment,
knowing there is no time pressure, people may move at a
very gradual pace and be more reluctant to bring certain
issues out into the open. The finality of limited sessions
can, in a sense, light a fire under people, providing an
impetus for jumping in and "getting down to business."

The way time limits are presented can make a difference.
Consider these two versions:

*"I know there is a lot going on in your life, and
I'm sorry, but in our clinic we can only offer 12
sessions. But I suggest we get started and see how
far we can get."*

*"Our clinic offers brief psychotherapy — which means
we see people for up to 12 sessions. We may not be
able to tackle all of the issues you have spoken to me
about, but I think we have a good opportunity to
work together and really focus on the most
important concerns you have."*

The first example is quite apologetic, while the second
example honestly acknowledges the limited sessions, while
accentuating the positive work that can be done.
Therapists must be able to be very honest and aboveboard
regarding all issues in therapy. We also have an obligation
to use approaches that maximize therapeutic leverage and
that instill realistic hopefulness.

Therapists' pessimism regarding outcomes from brief
therapy often accounts for a lack of enthusiasm and/or an
apologetic tone as the stage for the treatment is set. How
we present treatment in the opening session can have a
direct impact on client motivation. One colleague of mine
is accustomed to asking:

"How soon would you like to be feeling better (or
coping more successfully)?" The answer was almost always,
"As soon as possible!" Therapist: "Good. In fact, in brief
therapy the intention is to work together actively to get
results as soon as possible."

As treatment progresses, it is important to keep some
focus on how much time remains. If the client does not
spontaneously mention it halfway through the allotted
number of sessions, it is generally wise for the therapist to
mention the amount of time remaining. This can then be
used as a springboard for talking about what has happened
so far in treatment, the remaining issues to be dealt with,
and any thoughts or feelings the person may be having
about the approaching termination of therapy. It is
certainly better to initiate some discussion of termination
well before the last two sessions, so that there can be ample
time to address any issues that the ending of therapy may
evoke.

## ❖ *Targeted Treatment Strategies*

Providing a supportive relationship and encouragement to talk may certainly be enough to facilitate healing or growth in some clients. However, as I've argued at length in this book, most often this is simply not enough. Likewise, with treatment that is very nondirective and without a specific focus, the client is likely to meander and may arrive at the termination date with many issues still unresolved. This is why specific, targeted intervention strategies are so essential if we hope to help clients in short-term therapy. Such targeted treatments may focus on particular symptom disorders (e.g., panic disorder) and make use of research-derived protocols, or they may be based on an assessment of key psychological liabilities, as outlined in this book. At the heart of targeted strategies is a clear idea about "what needs to happen" and an approach that requires the therapist to be active.

## ❖ *Homework*

Taking on specific tasks between sessions — homework assignments — has been found to be an important part of successful brief therapy (see Appendix A). Such homework may include the practicing of assertive behavior, writing in a personal journal, or keeping records of negative cognitions.

The goals of homework include the following: (1) By actively engaging in tasks between sessions, the client can build on progress made during sessions; (2) It affords opportunities to rehearse, practice, and get feedback, strengthening the learning of new coping skills; (3) It gives support to the client for doing a fair amount of work on his/her own (encouraging autonomy). (4) It can help the client to solidify coping skills that can to be useful after therapy has ended.

##  *Developing Additional Sources of Support*

Many people who have gone through brief psychotherapy come to learn of the value of interpersonal support and emotional sharing. For many, it may be wise to look into various support groups as an ongoing resource after therapy ends. For some clients, the experience in brief therapy may convince them that they want or need to become involved in longer-term psychotherapy, geared to deal with issues that have not been adequately addressed in shorter-term treatment. For some clients this clearly can be seen as a positive outcome of brief therapy.

And finally, let's consider that the fact that coping, healing, and growth is never time-limited. It will continue to be a part of living for all of us. Brief therapy is simply an important experience encountered along the way, a time to interact with and benefit from a relationship with a guide (who happens also to be a fellow traveler).

The advent of the brief therapy movement has spawned the development of a number of new therapeutic models and innovative treatment strategies. One clear outcome is that nowadays more people have access to and are receiving mental health services than ever before. Many people clearly do benefit from time-limited psychotherapy. And a number of clients are experiencing more rapid relief from emotional suffering. For this I am grateful. It behooves all therapists to learn as much as we can about effective treatment strategies so we can offer our best to clients seeking psychotherapy.

At the same time, it is clear that many people who come to us are suffering from disorders that cannot be adequately addressed by brief therapy approaches. While I advocate shorter-term therapy in general, it would be foolish to think even for a moment that all psychiatric disorders could somehow be amenable to brief treatment. That idea is just as absurd as the notion that all medical illnesses can be addressed by way of time-limited outpatient treatment. I believe that, as mental health professionals, we have a moral obligation to step forward and speak out about what is clinically necessary treatment, and not be bashful about criticizing inappropriate health care policies. We must steadfastly bring pressure to bear on health care policy makers by stating the facts about the benefits as well as the limitations of mental health treatment. We must become advocates for those people suffering from more severe or chronic mental illnesses.

# "Homework" That Helps

There are several easy things a client can do between sessions that can help a lot to speed up the process of therapy. These simple strategies have been developed, tested out and found to be quite effective for people going through a wide array of difficult times. Here are a few examples of specific "homework" strategies.

### ❖ What Works and What Doesn't?

Often during times of stress, people conclude "nothing I do seems to help." But that's rarely true. Some actions do help, if only a little. It's important to try to discover any clues to why things do go well — "What made this possible?... what did I say or do, what did someone else say or do that really made a difference?" — and to jot down in a notebook 'things that help' and 'things that work'. Many people, to their surprise, discover that there already are some things they do that succeed in reducing distress or minimizing conflicts. These are strengths the client can build on!

At least, suggests Psychiatrist Gorden Deckert, when a problem-solving approach doesn't work, stop and take a close look at what you're doing that *doesn't* work and, at the very least, don't do *that!*

### ❖ Positive Activity Diary

People who feel overwhelmed or depressed tend to overlook or minimize their accomplishments. Such a person may get to the end of the day and conclude: "That day was wasted. I got nothing done." This perception increases feelings of low self-esteem and a sense of defeat. An activity diary can help present a more realistic view of events.

For at least one day, the client's assignment is to write down everything she does, even small things like picking up a toy or getting a drink for one of her children. Most people are surprised how busy they are from morning until night, and how much they get done.

A practical approach is to record the major events of each day in a small notebook: tasks completed; progress made on tasks, compliments received; a nice lunch with a friend; getting a letter; feeling good about a job well done; experiences that matter. The process works best if kept simple and easy. It is best to jot down only very brief three-to-five word statements. Then, review the list at the end of the day. Even very distressed people who feel as though they accomplished absolutely nothing in a day are often surprised to find out that in fact they have done many things or experienced some moments of pleasure. This approach is very easy to put into action and can give immediate pay-offs. It is an important way to avoid feelings of helplessness and low self-esteem.

### ❖ *Keeping Perspective*

Another homework project that often is helpful is to make a list of "things that matter." In the midst of hard times, it's so easy to focus mainly on bad stuff, and to lost sight of positive aspects of life. Here's an example from a college professor:

Things That Matter to Me:
1. My relationship with my kids
2. My teaching job; how I impact my students
3. My involvement in church
4. Reading exciting novels
5. Listening to my favorite music
6. Sailing
7. Exercising at the Y
8. Talking to my sister on the phone
9. Writing to or calling old friends
10. Driving in the country on a sunny day
11. Knowing I am a decent person, a good Dad
12. My sense of humor.

Adapted with permission from Preston, et al., *Every Session Counts* (1995)

# REFERENCES ❖

Alexander, F. and T. French (1946) *Psychoanalytic Therapy.* New York: Ronald.

American Psychiatric Association (1994) *Diagnostic and Statistical Manual of Mental Disorders,* Fourth Edition, Washington, D.C.: American Psychiatric Association.

Avis, H. (1993) *Drugs and Life.* Dubuque, Iowa: W.C. Brown and Benchmark.

Bandura, A. (1986) *Social Foundations of Thought and Action: A Social Cognitive Theory.* Englewood Cliffs, N.J.: Prentice-Hall.

Beck, A.T. (1976) *Cognitive Therapy and the Emotional Disorders.* New York: New American Library.

Bellak, L., M. Hurvich, and H.K. Gedimen (1973) *Ego Functions in Schizophrenics, Neurotics, and Normals: A Systematic Study of Conceptual Diagnostic and Therapeutic Aspects.* New York: John Wiley and Sons.

Bugental, J.F.T. (1995) Resistance. *Evolution of Psychotherapy Conference.* Las Vegas, Nevada.

Burns, D.D. (1980) *Feeling Good: The New Mood Therapy.* New York: The American Library, Inc.

Chessick, R. (1969) *How Psychotherapy Heals.* New York: Jason Aronson.

Chessick, R. (1974) *The Technique and Practice of Intensive Psychotherapy.* New York: Jason Aronson.

Elliott, C.H. and M.K. Lassen (1998) *Why Can't I Get What I Want.* Palo Alto, CA: Davies-Black Publishing.

Epstein, S. (1994) Integration of the cognitive and the psychodynamic unconscious. *American Psychologist, 49,* 709-724.

Frank, J. (1973) *Persuasion and Healing.* Baltimore: Johns Hopkins University Press.

Frey, W.H., C. Hoffman-Ahern, et al. (1983) Crying behavior in the human adult. *Integrative Psychiatry, 1:* 94-100.

Greenberg, L.S., L.N. Rice, and R. Elliott (1993) *Facilitating Emotional Change: The Moment-by-Moment Process.* New York: Guilford Press.

Horowitz, M.J. (1976) *Stress Response Syndromes.* New York: Jason Aronson.

Horowitz, M.J., C. Marmar, et al. (1984) *Personality Styles and Brief Psychotherapy*. New York: Basic Books.

Izard, C.E. (1971) *The Face of Emotion*. New York: Appleton-Century-Crofts.

Janoff-Bulman, R. (1992) *Shattered Assumptions*. New York: Free Press.

Johnson, S.M. (1985) *Characterological Transformations*. New York: W.W. Norton and Co.

Kelly, E.W. (1997) Relationship-centered counseling: A humanistic model of integration. *Journal of Counseling and Development, 75,* 337-345.

Kopp, S. (1992) *Blues Ain't Nothing But a Good Soul Feeling Bad*. New York: Simon and Schuster.

Marmar, C.R. (1991) Grief and bereavement after traumatic loss. *Audio Digest Psychiatry, 20,* No. 5.

Masterson, J.F. (1986) *The Real Self*. New York: Masterson Group, P.C.

Meisels, Murray (1988) A critique and redefinition of resistance in psychoanalysis. Address, American Psychological Association. Washington, D.C.

Michaels, R. (1990) Resistance in Therapy. *Audio Digest Psychiatry, 19,* No. 19.

Nisbett, R.E., D. Caputo, et al. (1973) Behavior seen as the actor and as seen by the observer. *Journal of Personality and Social Psychology, 27,* 154-164.

Peck, M.S. (1978) *The Road Less Traveled*. New York: Simon and Schuster, Inc.

Preston, J.D. (1993) *Growing Beyond Emotional Pain*. San Luis Obispo, CA: Impact Publishers.

Preston, J.D. (1996) *You Can Beat Depression* (Second Edition). San Luis Obispo, CA: Impact Publishers.

Preston, J.D. (1997) *Shorter-Term Treatments For Borderline Personality Disorders*. Oakland: New Harbinger.

Preston, J.D., J. O'Neal, and M. Talaga (1997) *Handbook of Clinical Psychopharmacology for Therapists*. Oakland, CA: New Harbinger.

Rogers, C.R. (1961) *On Becoming A Person*. Boston: Houghton Mifflin.

Seligman, M.E.P. (1990) *Learned Optimism*. New York: Pocket Books.

Shapiro, D. (1989) *Psychotherapy of Neurotic Character*. New York: Basic Books.

Shapiro, F. (Ed.) (1995) *Eye Movement Desensitization and Reprocessing: Basic Principles, Practices, and Procedures*. New York: Guilford Press.

Sifneos, P.E. (1979) *Short-Term Psychotherapy: Evaluation and Technique*. New York: Plenum.

Silk, K.R. (Ed.) (1994) *Biological and Neurobehavioral Studies of Borderline Personality Disorder*. Washington, D.C.: American Psychiatric Press.

Stiles, W.B., M. Startup, et al. (1996) Therapist intentions in cognitive-behavioral and psychodynamic-interpersonal psychotherapy. *Journal of Counseling Psychology, 43*, 402-414.

Stone, M.H. (1980) *The Borderline Syndromes: Constitution, Personality, and Adaptation*. New York: McGraw-Hill.

Strupp, H.H. (1969) Toward a specification of teaching and learning in psychotherapy. *Archives of General Psychiatry, 21*, 203-212.

Strupp, H.H., and Binder, J.L. (1984) *Psychotherapy in a New Key*. New York: Basic Books.

Thorbeck, J. (1993) Resistance in psychotherapy. *Practical Reviews in Psychiatry, 17*, No. 2.

Tomkins, S.S. (1962) *Affect, Imagery and Consciousness*. New York: Springer Publishing Co.

van der Kolk, B.A., A.C. McFarlane, and L. Weisaeth (Ed.) (1996) *Traumatic Stress*. New York: The Guilford Press.

Weiss, J. (1971) The emergence of new themes: A contribution to the psychoanalytic theory of therapy. *International Journal of Psychoanalysis, 52*, 459-4616.

Winnicott, D.W. (1958) *Collected Papers*. New York: Basic Books.

Young, J.E. (1994) *Cognitive Therapy For Personality Disorders: A Schema-Focused Approach*. Sarasota, Florida: Professional Resource Press.

Young, J.E. and Klosko, J.S. (1993) *Reinventing Your Life*. New York: Dutton Books.

# Index